WEALTHOLOGY

them back is second to none. She is the queen of this work and I wouldn't miss this book for anything.

— **Sean Patrick,** *That Guy Who Loves The Universe*

Michelle Lowbridge is quite simply a magician. Her energy process to clearing out literally any blocks within minutes is nothing short of a miracle, but it's her practical and humorous application that has me, and subsequently my clients, hiring her time and time again. In *Wealthology* she not only shares her wisdom and process, but has given coaches a viable tool to help raise the wealth consciousness of their clients. This is not so much a book that will be read once, but is a book that can sit on your desk as a reference tool to help yourself and others fundamentally shift their relationship to abundance, prosperity and wealth.

— **Stacy Nelson**, Bestselling author of
Your Inner Council & Writing the Damn Book

Creating wealth is and always has been an inner game and is one that Michelle Lowbridge intimately understands. *Wealthology* is full of deep, life-altering insights that have the ability to radically shift your energy and story around money in the best way possible. If you are looking to redefine your relationship with money and create room in your life for significantly more from a place of ease, effortlessness and abundance, this is the place to start.

— **Justin Faerman**, Co-Founder, *Conscious Lifestyle Magazine*

Wealthology is a powerful insight into how to unblock entrepreneurs' wealth streams and allow them to fully recognise their potential. It's for coaches who feel their clients' frustrations and gives key help to guide them to reaching their goals and aspirations.

— **Nick Ede**, CEO, EastofEden London

Finally! *Wealthology...* a DREAM resource both for myself and my clients!

As a business coach, the success of what I do is directly related to the amount of money my clients make as a result of my coaching. Over and over again, I have hit roadblock in my business as it quickly becomes apparent that my clients often have a damaged relationship with money.

As a business coach, I pride myself on teaching effective systems and processes. However, execution of my coaching is extremely difficult (if not impossible) when my clients do not believe they are worth the amount of personal wealth they desire, or they do not believe that abundance is available to them, and in most cases they significantly undervalue their time.

Wealthology could not have landed on my desk at a better time. As soon as I made my way through the manual, I knew this would be the solution to what has been a missing link in my coaching business for a long time! It is a dream to offer my clients a resource that will undoubtably change the game and allow me to have an even greater impact as a coach.

I can get so excited when I think about the transformations and ah-ha moments available to my clients as a result of adopting the Wealthology system because I know how greatly this will impact their success, their profits and their lives! The teachings in this book really should be a mandatory support resource to every coach working with entrepreneurs across all industries, a game changer!

Thank you Michelle for your commitment to impact in your work, it's refreshing!

—**Stephanie Joanne**, Online Brand
& Business Coach to Entrepreneurs

Wealthology is a must read for anyone interested in the psychology of money. Michelle Lowbridge really breaks down, in easy to understand terms, the blockages that hold us back from the money and success we aspire to. In fact, anyone who reads it will most definitely come away with a much better understanding of their relationship to money. A wealth of information, I found it to be one "AHA" moment after the next.

— **Pat Takaya Solomon**, director of *Finding Joe*

As a business mentor for women I see many 'money blocks' in my clients that prevent them from taking action and becoming as successful as I know they can. For me as their mentor it's frustrating to give them the tools but see them do nothing with them - out of fear. I've resisted bringing up money blocks with my clients because most of the information about money blocks is very fluffy and rather 'woo woo' - something that does not match my personality or teaching style at all. But Michelle's approach is logical and strategic - a breath of straightforward fresh air! I couldn't stop reading. I even discovered myself in a couple of the 'themes'. As a logical action-taking woman I'm grateful to Michelle for creating a book which takes different approach to prosperity and money blocks - an approach I'd be overjoyed to share with my clients.

—**Star Khechara**, Business & Fame Strategist, author of *The Facelift Diet*

This book is written by one of the most real, authentic, sincere, caring human beings I have met and known. The first time I connected over Skype with Michelle, she blew me away with the insights and knowledge she gave me regarding my Real Estate workshop and why it was mostly attended by men. This book is nothing like other books you read about wealth, it is very unique. *Wealthology* is a book based on real life stories with real people getting amazing results and transformation, almost immediately unlike the common wealth-building ways. In my opinion, *Wealthology* is not a book - it's like a manual that you can return to many times.

YOU owe it to yourself and the people you care for to read this book and learn from Michelle so you can help them - and YOU get to build a business for your self while doing that.

—**Tahani Aburaneh**, Amazon
Bestselling author of *Real Estate Riches*

I've always been fascinated with the role our sub-conscious patterns have in our daily lives. This is the first time I've read a book that so perfectly explains the connection between our limiting beliefs and wealth creation. If you want to unlock the door to your money prison, this book is the key.

—**Giovanni Marsico**, author of *The Gifted Entrepreneur*
and *Superhero Talent Scout at Archangel*

WEALTHOLOGY

THE SCIENCE OF SMASHING MONEY BLOCKS

MICHELLE LOWBRIDGE

NEW YORK

NASHVILLE • MELBOURNE • VANCOUVER

WEALTHOLOGY
THE SCIENCE OF SMASHING MONEY BLOCKS

© 2017 MICHELLE LOWBRIDGE

Published in New York, New York, by Morgan James Publishing. Morgan James and The Entrepreneurial Publisher are trademarks of Morgan James, LLC. www.MorganJamesPublishing.com

The Morgan James Speakers Group can bring authors to your live event. For more information or to book an event visit The Morgan James Speakers Group at www.TheMorganJamesSpeakersGroup.com.

ISBN 978-1-68350-263-0 paperback
ISBN 978-1-68350-264-7 eBook
Library of Congress Control Number: 2016916241

Shelfie

A **free** eBook edition is available with the purchase of this print book.

CLEARLY PRINT YOUR NAME ABOVE IN UPPER CASE

Instructions to claim your free eBook edition:
1. Download the Shelfie app for Android or iOS
2. Write your name in **UPPER CASE** above
3. Use the Shelfie app to submit a photo
4. Download your eBook to any device

Cover Design by:
Heidi Miller

Cover artwork:
Ruth Ridgeway

Interior Design by:
Bonnie Bushman

Editing:
Cynthia Kane

Author's photo courtesy of:
Peter Lowbridge

In an effort to support local communities, raise awareness and funds, Morgan James Publishing donates a percentage of all book sales for the life of each book to Habitat for Humanity Peninsula and Greater Williamsburg.

Get involved today! Visit
www.MorganJamesBuilds.com

DISCLAIMER

To preserve the anonymity and privacy of some of the individuals described in this book, the author has changed names and identities. This book is a reflection of the opinions of the author. Although every effort is made to teach the reader about smashing money blocks, there is no guarantee of results. The author and publisher do not assume and hereby disclaim any liability to any party for any loss, damage, or disruption caused by errors or omissions, whether such errors or omissions result from negligence, accident, or any other cause. The author and publisher are not liable or responsible for a reader's, or a reader's clients', subsequent financial misfortune, emotional distress or other subsequent occurrences in the life of the reader or their clients.

This Book does not provide legal, tax, accounting or financial advice and the information provided to reader and reader's clients is not intended as such. Reader and reader's clients should refer all legal, tax, accounting and financially related inquiries to appropriately qualified professionals.

DEDICATION

For Peter, which means rock. And he is, and he does.

TABLE OF CONTENTS

INTRODUCTION

It's no fun working with a client who isn't moving forward and stepping into the great potential that you know is waiting for them. Slow progress isn't good for your client, and it's not good for your reputation either. Clients who aren't getting great results probably aren't saying great things about you, and they're certainly not generating referrals for your business.

This means you have to spend more time on marketing and working on the business, than you get to spend actually serving clients and doing what you love to do, which is helping people!

Sometimes the hardest part of coaching is knowing when to coach and when to hold space for your client to make their own discoveries. If you spend too much time talking, the client switches off and isn't part of the journey. If the client spends a lot of time talking about something that isn't actually relevant, guess what? They don't move forward. This book gives you clear suggestions for the direction in which to focus your client's attention, so that you can easily guide them to their own revelations.

Feeling like you're failing at helping your clients is heartbreaking. You want to do a brilliant job, that's why you do it. If they hit upon a block that you don't have any experience with, or they have a pattern that you don't understand, it can be stressful to feel like you're 'winging' it as you try to guide them through. Feeling like a fraud is no fun at all, and can be really damaging to your confidence and ability to grow your business.

Wealthology® is here to help. Understanding the science of smashing money blocks will give you clear insights into your clients' inner programming, enabling you to confidently figure out why they're not making strides in their business, and what you can do about it.

WHY AM I WRITING THIS BOOK?

I know how it feels to run a service-based business and not have clients banging down the door for my help. I also know how it feels to be able to bring about such powerful changes, so rapidly, that the word-of-mouth generator kicks in, and you have more clients than you can cope with. I now work from my home office in the English countryside, using Skype to help clients all over the world, and people have flown from the other side of the globe to train in my Energy Editing® methodology. (By the way, being from England means some of my spelling might be different to what you're used to. This book isn't full of typos. Here, it really is enrol, colour, realise, recognise, honour, endeavour, and many others.)

A wise man told me a few months ago that I can't help everyone. To be honest, I was a bit annoyed by that. As an ego-driven human, I felt that he wasn't recognising my obvious magnificence. And then I realised I was being a dick, and listened to what he had to say.

He was right. The best way for me to help more people is to help the people who help people. To share what I know with coaches, so that their work becomes more powerful, and brings about faster transformation for their clients. That's the ripple effect, and I'm excited to be part of it.

WHO IS IT FOR?

This book is for coaches who work with entrepreneurs. The Wealthology principles can be used by anyone, however this book is really geared towards helping coaches to help their clients get faster results in growing their business. It's for the coach who feels their clients' sadness and frustration, and wishes there was more they could do. It's for the coach who has lived their client's journey, and sees the end result, but can't always identify with everything their clients say. For the coach who has a client who goes round in circles, and would do anything to know what's keeping them stuck in the loop. For the coach who has a client who keeps stumbling over invisible blocks.

Essentially, it's for the coach who's open to learning a fast way of identifying how their clients are blocking money, and wants to add a unique way of smashing those blocks to their toolbox. If you're reading this to find out more about your own money blocks, fantastic! Get ready for some great insights into your relationship with money. This is no-nonsense self-development, and I admire you for being here.

WHAT ARE MONEY BLOCKS?

A money block is something that stops us from being able to make, create, enjoy, save, spend and manage money.

What we tend to see are symptoms of money blocks: Not enough income, too many outgoings, debts, business that's slow, a general lack of enjoyment, that there are things we want to do that we can't afford to do, there are things we want for our family that we can't pay for, we don't like dealing with money and it stresses us out. We make poor decisions about money.

These are symptoms of money blocks. So if you're working with somebody and they are struggling to get to the next step in their business, and they're being blocked from taking action, marketing their work, having clarity, or they do all these things and the money still doesn't show up, these are signs that demonstrate what's going on in their relationship with money. They are signs that there are money blocks.

WHERE ARE THE ACTUAL MONEY BLOCKS?

If you trace behind the symptoms you'll find the conscious thinking. If you sink below that you'll find some subconscious thinking, which is the monkey mind whispering all sorts of negativity, and keeping your client on the wrong track. There are lots of things you can do to work with the conscious mind, things like journaling, mindset work, thought-reprogramming. And it can be a very slow process.

You can also work with the subconscious. There are ways of working to change subconscious thought patterns. It might take a little less time, depending on the tool that you have. Both of these approaches, whilst they have their merits, are slow, can be hard work, can take months of dedication to have an effect, and generally you need to keep applying them to keep seeing the benefits.

However, if you sink below the subconscious, you find the energy system. The energy system feeds the subconscious, and the conscious mind. If you eliminate a problem from the subconscious, without dealing with it in the energy system, it's likely to come back. Some energy-work modalities don't deal with the full energy system, they only work in one part of it, so again, problems seem to reoccur, whereas really, they were never fully eliminated in the first place.

Clearing money blocks without working in the full energy system is like trimming the heads off weeds in the garden. It looks better temporarily but the problem will keep coming back until you pull out the roots. Don't attempt to do healing or energy work on your clients, or try to release fears, beliefs and emotions, or trigger old pain, if you are not trained to do so. It's not fair to your clients to 'have a go'. If you can't do the work effectively and efficiently, direct them to someone who can help.

UNDERSTANDING THE SCIENCE OF SMASHING MONEY BLOCKS

Not all money blocks are obvious. It might be that your client has a deep-rooted belief that 'money is evil', however it's often the case that what's limiting their relationship with wealth, is about something else, apparently unrelated.

My friend Giovanni Marsico gives a brilliant analogy of your client as a superhero, with a unique superpower that can help many people. Every superhero has his or her individual kryptonite. Something that, no matter what they do, it triggers their weaknesses, makes them helpless, and stops them from using their superpower. This kryptonite is a combination of thought processes, fears, and beliefs about certain things. For example, if, as a child, your client was punished for expressing their personality, it creates a stressful memory that is stored in the energy system. The energy system then tells the subconscious mind to prevent that traumatic experience from happening again. So, as an adult entrepreneur, when the next step up in their business means expressing their personality, it triggers the old stress in their energy, the subconscious goes into protection-mode, and they are completely unable to take effective action. They either stop moving forward, or they do so under extreme stress. To the untrained eye, it doesn't seem like it has anything to do with money, yet it completely blocks them from easily creating wealth.

Smashing money blocks from the energy system is like identifying your client's kryptonite, hunting it down and eliminating it. Without these invisible triggers, clients evolve into the superheroes they are born to be, help the people they are here to help, and easily create the wealth they deserve, so that they can enjoy the freedom it brings and experience the fullness of their dreams and desires.

WHERE DO I START LOOKING FOR THESE BLOCKS?

That's exactly what this book is for. The Wealthology system gives you a way of identifying how your client relates to money - their Wealthology Profile - and the exact places to find their money blocks - the Wealthology Themes. By cross-referencing your client's profile with each money block theme, you have a complete guide to how, why and where they're blocking money, and what to do about it.

When you can't see what a block is, it's a lot harder to smash it – conversely, when you can rapidly hone in on an issue, you can get straight to work on helping to sort it out. Being a coach is a tough gig if you can't create rapid change. In this fast-evolving world, clients expect equally fast transformation. People are waking up, they want to run their own businesses, to live on purpose, to enjoy wealth, to find love, and they don't see why they should have to wait. They hire a coach and they expect miracles. With this book in your toolbox, you won't disappoint them.

You'll do better work. You'll achieve faster results. Your clients will trust you, and more than that, they will love and appreciate you. And then something magical happens: they'll start talking about you. They'll recommend you to their friends and acquaintances. Your name will crop up in conversations happening on the other side of the world. You get to serve more and more people!

There are so many reasons this is great news...

The magic: You get to show up and work your magic, and fulfil your purpose. You get to help clients eliminate the mysterious blocks that have always tripped them up, so they can leap forward, and in this line of work there is nothing more rewarding.

The ripple effect: The people you help go out and help other people! The higher level you serve at, the more your clients are able to go out and serve *their* clients and customers. The ripple effect extends far outside business; when you help other people to light up they spread love and happiness in their lives too. There really is no limit on how far-reaching the results of your work are.

The success: Life gets a lot simpler when you're in alignment, and creating clients through referrals. The money, time and energy you spend on marketing is dramatically reduced. You don't have to have complicated funnels or hold icky sales calls. You just show up as you, and help the people you most enjoy helping. Simple.

The wealth: Today, entrepreneurs want fast transformation, and when you can provide it, you are valuable. Clients want to work with you. Your business grows, and you're able to create wealth for yourself and your loved ones. Money means freedom, choices, and time to spend doing the things you love with the people you love.

HOW WILL THIS BOOK HELP YOU?

This book provides two resources.

- The Wealthology Profile is a way of understanding your clients, which gives key insights about the emotional patterns, triggers, and behaviours that block them from money and success. If you'd like to know your Profile, go to www.michellelowbridge. com/wealthology-quiz/ and identify it with 11 easy questions.
- The Wealthology Themes are 12 core areas to look at with your clients, to help you quickly identify where your client is stuck. These Themes are a unique approach to understanding money blocks, and the book cross references each one with each Profile, offering you crucial information about why your client is blocked, and what you can do to help.

There are suggestions for how to help your clients at every stage, enabling you to better use all the existing tools in your toolbox. You'll find a **free Wealthology Toolkit** at www.michellelowbridge.com/ wealthologygifts. It contains lots of resources, including my Limiting Belief Release technique to clear limiting beliefs in 30 seconds. (Think E.F.T on steroids, as one of my certified Energy Editing Professionals calls it.)

Time and time again I've created such rapid transformations for my clients that within days (and sometimes hours) they've seen a substantial increase in their income. I'd like you to do the same for your clients, so shall we get started?

Let's meet the six types of clients that you work with.

THE WEALTHOLOGY PROFILES

THE ACHIEVER

Attracts money with the energy of fulfilment, and is always striving to reach a level where they feel accomplished with their abilities, skills and self-development. The Achiever gets blocked when they don't feel that their current abilities are worthy of abundance.

THE STRATEGIST

Attracts money with a 'driven' energy, and is fuelled by a love of targets, goals and strategies. The Strategist needs to know outcomes before they take action, and they block money by controlling too much.

1

THE HUSTLER

Attracts money with a fierce energy, because they're determined to prove themselves. They often don't realise that they're always battle-ready. The Hustler gets blocked by denying that they're in pain and not healing old wounds.

THE GUARDIAN

Attracts money with the energy of enthusiasm, and being positive and excited about their ideas. They focus lots of their energy on other people's dreams and achievements. The Guardian gets blocked by constantly managing other people's emotions.

THE THINKER

Attracts money by feeling worthy of it, and constantly self-assesses whether what they are doing is valuable. They think they can only create wealth in a 'proper' job. The Thinker gets blocked when they don't see the worthiness of their inner dreams and big ideas.

THE LIGHT

Attracts money by radiating brilliance and being a messenger of their truth. They spend a lot of energy stressing about what other people think of them. The Light gets blocked by worrying about outshining others and leaving them behind.

There you have them, the six Wealthology Profiles, and how they attract money and create wealth. There's so much more to discover about each one, so now I'd like to show you where to look, so you can identify what's blocking your clients from greater success.

Money blocks aren't just about money. They come in all sorts of disguises, which is why so many people struggle to get wealth flowing to them consistently in return for doing what they love.

Each of the following chapters describes an area that frequently throws up problems for your clients, many of which are places that other coaches just aren't looking: Family, Loneliness, Living on Purpose, Self-Disapproval, Higher Self, Controlling, Self-Punishment, Anger, Encouragement, Self-Actualisation, Abundance, and Self-Liberation.

Give yourself the edge, and create more success for your own business, by using this guide to speed up your clients' transformations. Bringing about rapid change and skyrocketing your clients' ability to make money is key to your success: it generates word-of-mouth marketing that money just can't buy, and it makes you valuable, which means you can expedite your profit potential and create services that are truly worth high-level investment.

Ready?

Wealthology Money Block:

FAMILY

I n March 2014 I quit practicing kinesiology.

After five years of studying, building my practice, and working with beloved clients, I packed away my kit to concentrate on my online business for the last few months of my third pregnancy.

I had worked through my feelings of guilt around quitting something I'd worked so long to get to the top of, and I was genuinely excited to focus on my happiness teaching and building a business that I could run from home.

A few months later, in late-July, baby Jackson was six weeks old and utterly perfect, being doted on by his dad and his two big sisters.

I, however, had started to feel restless.

I had heard of the concept of 'money blocks' – the idea that on some level we block money and resist it. And I kept feeling called to read a book called The Big Leap, by Gay Hendricks, but I'd been putting it off.

Resisting a book about resistance. Ironic.

Finally, with my intuition screaming in my ears to just pick up the book, I grabbed it and started reading. Hendricks explains that we all have a level of what we subconsciously believe we deserve to have and earn in life, and when we bump against those levels and try to push past them, we meet resistance.

We self-sabotage. We attract circumstances that make things difficult – and so we end up staying at the same level, energetically – and financially. When I read that part, my intuitive bells started chiming on full alert. This simple theory explained why, in my two businesses – an online retail store and my kinesiology practice – when one got busy the other one slowed right down. I had an invisible limit on my income, and no matter how hard I worked the total income would remain the same.

It explained why at the end of my honeymoon I manifested a jellyfish sting and then put my back out - because the resort was more luxurious than I was used to and so I couldn't possibly just relax and enjoy it. It explained why if I managed to squirrel away some extra savings, then the washing machine or car would break, because I couldn't possibly have that much security. And of course, if everything started going really well, if I dared to think about how well things were going, I'd wake up the next morning with my skin breaking out. Lovely.

Skin issues aside, my invisible money limit had ensured that my income had stayed almost exactly the same for three years. It seemed I needed to go on a massive money mindset mission to root through my mind and psyche for the secret explanation for my attitude to money. Then I remembered - I'm a Kinesiologist! I don't need to wait, I can just ask my subconscious for the answers.

So I did.

I found my first money limiting block in about two minutes. No exercises, no depressing moments, no tears, I just did The Energy Editor® thing and muscle tested for the answers. In the energy work I do, all problems have a related block in the energy system. And what did the testing reveal? That my invisible money limit, the subconscious belief that was keeping me at a low income, was all to do with the two sides of my family.

One side: well-off, miserable, and legendary for their tight-fistedness. The other side: hard-working, less well-off, great fun, super-loving, really happy, and heart-breakingly generous. My experiences growing up with these two influences had resulted in a rather faulty belief – all rich people are miserable, and if you want to be really happy, don't earn lots of money.

So, problem found, only a few months of mindset work to fix it, according to the book. Ugh. That sounded like hard work. Then I remembered - I'm a Kinesiologist! I can fix this right now. So I did. A few Energy Edits later and I'd shifted my first money block. It would turn out to be the most important and life-changing thing I'd done since saying to my husband, Pete: "I'm VERY broody." (Translation: Make me pregnant, NOW.)

Within 48 hours everything had transformed. Having driven my 'well-loved' Corsa for ten years, I went out the next day and bought a new car, which I also manifested a £5000 discount on. I found a solution to a long-standing financial problem. This problem did not have a solution, yet somehow I found one. This was exciting stuff and I wanted to share it.

The next day I popped into a Facebook group: "I've got 15 baby-free minutes, and a new skill to practice. Does anyone want a money block found and corrected? I'm a Kinesiologist and I'll tune into your energy system and muscle test to find it, and then I'll clear it for you." The crowd, as they say, went wild. Fifteen minutes ended up being two hours, with a pause to feed the baby and coming back for another few hours.

Now, when I first joined this group, as a way of getting to know people I'd offered to find their biggest money block for them, using my muscle testing magic. I got to know ladies in there and I got a big response. But this time, because my hidden money story had changed, something else happened:

"I want to book a session with you Michelle."

"I want a private session Michelle, how can we do that?"

"Can you and I work together one-on-one, Michelle?"

I explained that I had a six week old baby, and also that I was no longer practicing.

"Well if you decide to come out of retirement please let me know."

"And me."

"Me too!"

I received private messages saying the same thing. So I spoke to Pete. He was a teacher, so he was around for the summer, and he was quite happy to be daddy daycare if I wanted to bust out my kinesiology kit and do some work. I knew there was one thing I was going to do differently. Part of the reason I'd closed my kinesiology practice was that it wasn't a sustainable business model. In theory, my price was meant to be £70 a session. In reality, it was usually anything from £20 to £40, with the average being £35. I gave discounts to mums, children, friends, friends of friends. I didn't like talking about money, I worried constantly about what people would think about me, and I didn't have the confidence to value my skills.

But now I felt different. My energy around money had completely shifted. I just didn't feel the same crippling fear around asking for money and charging my worth. I said to Pete: "I'm willing to do the work, but there's no way I'm going to do it at low prices, especially as it's summer. If I'm going to be away from you and the baby and the girls then I'm going to say it's £100 a session. At that price it will feel really good. Can you imagine if someone actually paid me £100?!" I had no expectation that anyone would sign up, but I posted in the group that the hubster was happy to hold the baby, and I could do some sessions and it was £100.

Within 24 hours I had 11 bookings. The following week I did 14 sessions. I made £1400. £1400!!! In a week? It was unheard of, crazy, exciting and mind-blowing. Not only that, but I got great feedback and amazing things started happening for the ladies who had a session with me.

They shared their experiences.

Things like:

"Since my session with Michelle… money is flowing in."

"Since my session… I was contacted by my ideal client a few hours later."

"Since my session… people are booking my VIP experience."

And I got busier and busier.

On the 20th of July I started taking bookings. By the 31st I'd received $5000 into my PayPal account. (I was charging in dollars as many of my clients are in the USA.) Zero to $5000 - in ELEVEN DAYS - from a business that I'd closed! And guess what? Even though one income stream went crazy, the other one didn't slow down. My online store was busier than ever too. I ended up having an $11,600 month - by far the most money I'd ever made.

There were a few hiccups as I smacked into my limits – the dryer immediately died and I threw water all over my laptop. A couple of Energy Edits (and a very tech-talented hubby) later and everything was fine again and I kept moving upward with no more problems. But that's not the end of the story. I thought I'd see what happened if I posted an offer of help in another – much larger - forum. Assuming there was no way the members would be interested, I sat back, ready to feel humiliated as my offer of free energy work was inevitably swept to the bottom of the page.

Instead, I found myself calling "PETE!! PETE I need your help!" And we spent the next four hours in a whirl of energetic excitement. I tested and set up the energy work, while he told me who was done and moved each set-up from my desk so I could do the next one. Five hundred and fifty-five comments on the thread later and there was no way I'd be able to do them all. The next day I had to admit defeat. However, I had an idea.

"If anyone is interested then I can do a group correction where I smash the same money block for everyone?"

And the crowd again went wild.

I was having a great time, people were feeling the energy shift, asking me how I did it, reporting back that good things were happening after my work, it was such good fun. So I posted another 'group correction' and it got another great response. That day I was having a chat with my friend Amy, telling her about the group work, and she uttered the immortal words:

"That's a product. Right there. That's a product."

And The Prosperity Prescription was born. Within 20 minutes she had me collecting email addresses from people who were interested in joining. People signed up for more information - I kept hitting refresh on the Mail Chimp page and I couldn't believe my eyes. On Friday the 8th of August, my existing list had 46 people on it. By Saturday the 9th of August my new list had 300 new names and it was still growing. That's 650% growth in my list in one day.

The countdown timer on my opt-in page was going to hit zero hour on Monday the 11th of August, meaning I had to launch a product (which didn't exist) in 72 hours. What a rush! Emails went out on Saturday and Sunday. On Sunday night my hubby built me a camera tripod out of a step-ladder, a ruler and some electrical tape and

I recorded the video that went on my sales page. On Monday, the video went out, Charter Members were invited to enrol and Pete and I sat with our daughters, wondering what would happen. I had said to them: "This might mean that Mummy gets paid to do something she absolutely loves doing! So cross your fingers."

And they did, sitting with their tiny fingers crossed and their enormous blue eyes staring at the screen.

We waited.

Then...

'Ping'

Email.

"Someone signed up! Someone signed up!"

We went crazy!

'Ping' again!

The girls cheered, I cried, Pete was stunned.

And so it went on.

We closed enrolment with 165 amazing Charter Members for The Prosperity Prescription. I have never been so humbled, so grateful, and so mind-blowingly honoured. I had created something and people wanted to join in. I had formed a group that would take its members on a journey of transformation over the next year. It was a dream come true – one of those dreams that's just so big, and so magical, and so life-changing, you don't even dare to dream it. It's just within you, waiting to be unleashed. And because my work these days is all about helping you and your clients achieve greatness, enjoy wealth and be comfortable around money, I'll tell you the numbers.

The Prosperity Prescription launch generated $45,267 in two weeks. Using a skill that, five weeks previously, I thought was redundant.

That's what happened to me when I found and smashed my money blocks around family 'stuff'.

Since then I've worked with hundreds of people to find their blocks to money and success. These blocks come in many guises, and eliminating them creates rapid transformation. I'm writing this book because I want you to be able to create the life of *your* dreams by helping your clients to create *theirs*.

What do you think would happen if you were able to identify and smash your clients' money blocks related to their family?

Shall we find out?

THE ACHIEVER

The Achiever worries about what their family members think of them, and also about what other people think of their family. Their relatives (especially the women) are often very fearful of doing anything that might give people a reason to talk about them. This is passed on to The Achiever who worries about doing anything that might upset the family, or attract attention. The family ethic is likely to be very grounded in hard work, so it can be hard for these clients to follow their heart and live in flow, enjoying doing what they love.

This affects their business because trying to build a life inside the tiny box called 'That which no-one will talk about' is not much fun, and they feel guilty about making changes in their life which might tear the box and rock the family boat, so they can feel very stuck.

Help your Achiever clients by releasing their fears around what happens when people talk about them. Release their belief that it's selfish to focus on their own dreams and goals, and help them clear the guilt associated with not doing what's expected of them.

Doing this work can be immensely freeing for The Achiever, and it might be the first time they're able to step out and do what they love without being crippled with fear about what other people think.

THE STRATEGIST

The Strategist always feels the need to be responsible. Even as the youngest family member, they will take responsibility for everyone else's problems. Their family often has really high expectations of them, and conversely they often have low expectations of other people.

This affects their business because they link their value to their capability. They worry that their worthiness relies upon their ability to take care of everyone and everything, and will massively over-commit, until they begin to resent their work. They find it hard to establish boundaries, and keep saying 'yes' until they're completely burnt out and fed up.

Help your Strategist clients by encouraging them to let other people show capability. To do this you will need to clear a fair amount of fears, especially as they tend to feel that people they don't take care of will leave. If you have the tools to do so, help them release the pain they carry, and look for areas of their life now where they can let other people share the weight.

When this block is cleared they'll be able to set boundaries without fearing that it diminishes their value. This will impact their business because they'll begin to have a healthier relationship with people they work with, and be able to command respect instead of feeling they have to over-earn it. They'll stop burning themselves out, and begin to find ways of working that feel good for them, with responsibility being shared with others.

THE HUSTLER

As a child, the Hustler often found themselves in trouble for voicing their opinions. They always had a feeling that they were different, and often spent a good chunk of their childhood waiting to become adults, so they could make their own choices. The kicker here is that family and approval are subconsciously far more important to them than they realise. Beneath the freethinking exterior is a big softie who would love nothing more than to be approved of and completely accepted.

This affects their business because they're subconsciously desperate for approval, which means they hold back, and carry unnecessary fear. This means that a lot of the time they're really stressed out, and it limits their ability to really connect with other people. They don't realise it but they're waiting for the day they accidentally say something wrong and everything comes crashing down around them.

Help your Hustler clients by going beneath their protective surface, to find and release the fears that they have hidden from themselves. It can be especially transformational to eliminate their need for approval from their family.

The impact of this work can mean that they're able to relax, and to step up to a new phase of their true selves, without fearing repercussions. This influences everything, from their marketing, to their daily enjoyment of their work, to the direction that their business is taking.

THE GUARDIAN

The Guardian feels they have to modify their behaviour to fit in. In childhood, they might have felt very confused as to why they weren't chosen, or why a sibling was a favourite, or why they were ignored. A small number of incidences where their enthusiasm for their own talents resulted in an adult losing their temper may have had a huge effect on their ability to be themselves.

This affects their business because they're often easily intimidated, and fear being judged or having love withdrawn if they're fully authentic.

This is really stressful for them because their very nature is to be excited and passionate. This means they tame their message, and tone down their truth, which limits their ability to connect with their audience and find their 'people'.

Help your Guardian clients by creating a safe space for the enormity of their passion, and for the depths of their anger. These clients have spent years keeping themselves on a narrow path, feeling that the extremes of their emotions and opinions are unacceptable. If you have the ability, help them to release their pent up frustrations and pain. Allow their fullest expression of themselves to emerge, and integrate the belief that whatever they're feeling is perfectly acceptable.

The impact of unleashing a Guardian client from their need to play it safe can be far-reaching. It allows them to fully step up, to fully own their passionate nature and to stop constantly managing other people's emotions.

THE THINKER

The Thinker was raised to have a strong sense of duty. This affects their ability to choose what feels best for themselves, and keeps them focused on doing the 'right' thing. They see keenly where others have tried hard or sacrificed for them, and they try very hard to clear this debt or repay their family in whatever way they can.

This affects their business because they're often doing something that they really don't want to do. They may well have a secret passion, or healing abilities that no one knows about, and often have the feeling that they are being called to do something that in some way will let other people down.

Help your Thinker clients by creating a safe space for them to explore their individuality, and celebrate it with them. Release their fears around being seen in their truth, and letting people down. Clear their stress and worries, without reflecting back to them a need to take action. Giving them a list of action steps is just giving them another duty to fulfil.

This will impact their business by opening them up to possibilities they really didn't know existed for them. Showing the Thinker that they are worthy of true happiness is like switching on a light inside them. They will begin to look at their wider options, and will benefit hugely from your encouragement, praise and celebration of the baby steps they feel ready to take.

THE LIGHT

The Light had to grow up fast and 'be good'. As children, they were often expected to be tiny adults, and spent a lot of their time trying very hard not to upset anyone. They often believe that their innate brightness somehow makes them less lovable – they must not outshine siblings, they must not show off, they must keep themselves dimmed and let other people take the spotlight.

This affects their business because they hold back their ideas, their brilliance, and their abilities. They're subconsciously convinced that being their true self will hurt other people, and invite punishment, so they feel they must be sensible, and do whatever they can to avoid making other people uncomfortable.

Help your Light clients by showing them that it's safe for them to reveal their light, their joy, and their brightness. Create a safe environment for them to really shine. Help them to release the sadness and the burdens of responsibility for other people's insecurities that were given to them as children. Clear the limiting beliefs and fears around being punished and forsaken.

This will have a great impact on their business, because the brightness that made their childhood difficult is their greatest gift as adults. They'll realise that showing up is not the same as showing off, and they'll attract opportunities, and really enjoy a great sense of freedom to be themselves.

Smashing my family money blocks led to me making $45, 267 in two weeks. If I hadn't edited my energy I would have continued repeating the same patterns, I'd probably still be making about $15,000 a year, and my husband would be stuck in a stressful teaching job. Imagine the breakthroughs your clients can get when you do this work!

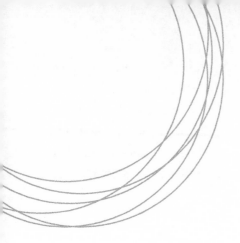

Wealthology Money Block:

LONELINESS

K ate came to me feeing very stressed about money. She described how she was able to show up on social media, being bright and present, and really shining, but as soon as it came to a money conversation: "My confidence completely dips, and I get really small." Something about asking for money literally made her feel like she was shrinking. Kate had a growing network of potential clients, was getting great engagement, and is extremely talented - but she was doing a lot of work for free, and struggling to make the transition to creating an income from what she loved to do. She'd had numerous conversations with people who were interested in working with her, yet when it came to the transaction, she felt completely unable to retain her 'brightness' and was unable to close the investment.

I started muscle testing and found that Kate had a strong subconscious belief that she was small, and that it meant she was going to get left behind. She had an equally powerful belief that if she released this belief and became powerful, that she would leave other people behind. These opposing beliefs meant that whatever Kate did, her subconscious told her that it would result in loneliness. As someone who holds connection as one of her highest values, this was extremely stressful, and kept her totally stuck.

Kate also had a limiting belief that she was ordinary, and that being ordinary meant, "I don't hurt anybody." We cleared all of these triggers from her energy system and subconscious.

Three weeks after we worked together, Kate felt completely different about talking about money, and was able to stand in her brightness and power in any situation. She booked her largest-ever client, made over $40,000 in one month, and had an amazing time celebrating with her family.

That's what happens when you smash your clients' blocks related to loneliness!

Loneliness is not an emotion; it's a state of being; a combination of isolation, disconnection and helplessness, and it's extremely stressful to the body, mind, and energy system. Most of your clients will have experienced loneliness, but they probably have no idea how much it affects their ability to make money and create success.

Periods of loneliness will have made them question their worth, doubt their likeability, damaged their confidence and made them feel like a failure. The ripple effect into their lives is huge, and they will often have subconsciously linked an element of success to being lonely. That's why this entire chapter is dedicated to helping people with their past pain related to loneliness. I can't promise this work will be easy. You might have to dig deep and hold space for your client to connect to some old pain, but if you're able to do that, it will be worth it.

Releasing the stress from loneliness will change your clients. When they drop this old baggage, and shed their heavy coat of protection, they travel lighter, shine brighter, and attract success and opportunities. This is how you can help them…

THE ACHIEVER

The Achiever fears what will happen to them if they don't follow the herd mentality. They have a subconscious belief that doing their own thing will result in complete isolation.

This affects their business because their own ideas get lost in the noise of other people's opinions, so they find it really hard to identify what they really enjoy, or stick with a project long enough to really get it going.

Help your Achiever clients by clearing their engrained sense of worry about being judged and rejected. Find their fears around needing to fit in, and release them. The ideal outcome for these clients as you work through loneliness is to bring them to a state of peace within themselves that doesn't depend on external factors.

This will have a great impact on their business because they'll start enjoying their own ideas and creating the freedom to develop them, without worrying what people think. They'll find everything in their business so much easier, including getting out of paralysis-mode and taking action, when you've cleared their blocks related to loneliness.

THE STRATEGIST

The Strategist gets blocked by loneliness because it's usually a deeply rooted theme in their lives. They have vivid memories of feeling lonely, and it's often an issue that's chased them into adulthood. They absolutely crave connection but they fear rejection so strongly that it often prevents them from taking the steps they know they need to take to relieve the loneliness.

This affects their business because they automatically plan ahead and try to anticipate the outcome of every situation. This is unfortunate, because others can sense the energy of their actions and it's often subconsciously misinterpreted as manipulation, which leads to people withdrawing or closing their hearts (and their wallets).

Work with your Strategist client to release the past pain of loneliness and to show them how they are worthy of heart connections. If you can do so delicately and with precision, without triggering all of their old pain, release the stress from their loneliness wounds.

This is essential work for these clients, and they'll start to feel a lot less helpless. Helplessness is a hugely stressful emotion, and releasing this and its links with loneliness can be absolutely transformative. They will stop needing so much control, see an upsurge in their confidence, and find it much easier to see the way forward, as well as being able to experience heart-connections.

THE HUSTLER

The Hustler thinks loneliness is a sign of weakness and failure. They will often identify as an outsider, and the very thought of 'needing' friends is a trigger that makes the walls come up. They often have memories of their confidence causing disconnection, leading to a tendency to prepare for adversity and to expect to be unaccepted.

This affects their business because Hustlers are not always sure who to trust as friends, advisors and their support. They often feel it safer to go it alone. They find it hard to build a team, and continue working solo long after their business is too big for them to do so easily.

Hustler clients need your help because they'll be the last ones to admit to being lonely. Clear their fear of being vulnerable or seen as a victim. They will admit to their failings only when they feel they have dealt with them, which gives an impression of openness that often hides great pain. If you have the tools and experience, find the root of the pain and clear it, so that they can begin to heal.

This will impact their business because they'll begin to cultivate stronger relationships and a real support system. Doing this will elevate the business in a way that allows them to truly serve with their gifts, rather than doing all the busy work.

THE GUARDIAN

The Guardian fears loneliness so much that they hold back and play small. They often believe it's inevitable when they show their true personality and feelings. Rejection after being misunderstood is a huge thing for these clients; it's often plagued them for an entire lifetime.

This affects their business because something as simple as posting on social media and not getting a great response can be very painful for them; they feel hurt and defeated and will return to being in the background.

Work with your Guardian clients to release the stress from their memories of feeling sad and alone. Only do this if you have tools and skills that allow you to release it gently and safely. Clear their limiting beliefs that being in the limelight will result in loneliness, and release their fears of not being understood.

This work will really allow The Guardian to enjoy their fullest expression of themselves. If you are able to do this work and then support them through the first steps of putting themselves out there, and strengthen them against the dip in courage that always follows their bold steps forward, you'll see a remarkable transformation.

THE THINKER

The Thinker feels that they don't fit in. This is often because they have a 'formal' side, which is often the side they use to make money, and then they have a hidden secret side, which is usually more 'alternative'. They've grown up feeling that there's something wrong with them, and on the outside of things.

This affects their business because they're rarely doing what they really love or using the gift that they have to share. Instead they do what is expected of them to maintain the illusion of avoiding loneliness.

Help your Thinker clients by releasing their past pain of feeling excluded, especially when they thought that it was somehow their fault. Being exiled from the tribe is a core fear for them. Release their limiting beliefs that they're not good enough, and the fear that their true self isn't worthy of love or money.

When you help The Thinker tap into the very core of themselves, they will start really sharing the truth of who they are. That fantastic breakthrough feels like a huge relief once it's done, and creates a wonderful ripple effect when they share their gift with other people.

THE LIGHT

The Light fears loneliness more than almost anything, and they will limit almost everything about themselves to avoid being lonely. These clients are fearful of being too much, too bright, too opinionated, too loud, too happy, and they feel that all of those things cause people to leave them. They've often been taught that vulnerability is a sign of weakness, or that 'people don't like weak people', so they tend to suffer in silence.

This affects their business because they feel very limited: they can't truly express themselves in the 'positive' and really shine, and they also can't truly express themselves in the 'negative' and be vulnerable. They get stuck, and hold themselves back, because then at least if they fail they know it's because they self-sabotaged.

Help your Light clients by holding space for them to shine. Release the pain of their past rejections if you have the tools to do so. Clear their fears and limiting beliefs that they can't shine without becoming lonely.

Doing this work means they can start showing up in the fullest expression of themselves, without fearing that there will be terrible consequences. This allows them to radiate brilliance and vulnerability, which massively heightens their ability to connect with their audience and expand their reach.

⌒⊙⊙⊙⊙⌒

Loneliness might not be the sexiest-sounding subject, however this is essential work, and the foundation for many money blocks. Get in there, heal the pain, and prepare strong new ground for your clients to build their successes on.

Wealthology Money Block:

LIVING ON PURPOSE

When Victoria came to see me, she was charging $3000 - $6000 for a package of coaching sessions. She was feeling very challenged by the amount of work involved in running the business, outside of the client work. She felt that what she was doing was making money, but that it was out of alignment with a message she wanted to share, and felt blocked from talking about. She wanted to step fully into her calling, and she was worried that it wouldn't work out financially. She had been struggling with this for several months, and was clearly overwhelmed. She was feeling very disillusioned, and wanted to charge more money and have fewer clients but couldn't see a way forward.

We began to release the stress around not knowing the outcome, and the fear of letting her guard down. Victoria had a belief that the formal business strategy she was using was keeping her 'safe', and that if she followed her heart she wouldn't make money. We quickly released that belief, and some accompanying fears. She had also subconsciously linked success from her calling, with the idea that 'then people will always be taking', and 'there will be pressure to be perfect'. We unlinked those concepts from each other. Finally, we released the belief that 'following my calling must be difficult' and cleared the emotional stress around being 'isolated'.

Victoria found the work emotional, and I advised her to take some time to rest and let the energy realign and assimilate the changes. Without all the blocks around her purpose, she was able to see the best way forward, make a few tweaks in her business, and a few weeks later, she closed her first $75,000 client. She wanted fewer clients, investing at a higher level, and that's what she got.

Purpose.

If your clients aren't connected to their purpose, they're living by accident. If they're not writing a story for their own lives, they're probably playing small parts in everyone else's. When your clients don't have a big goal, they're likely to be easily distracted. And if there are things blocking them from their purpose, they're likely to feel stressed out, overwhelmed, and unhappy.

When you're not concentrating on your purpose, success is hollow, and life is shallow. It's so easy to be thrown off track, and it leads to confusion, misery and inner turmoil.

Each type of client has a unique set of demons that distract them from their purpose.

This is what those demons look like, and why they're bad for business.

THE ACHIEVER

The Achiever gets distracted from their purpose because they feel they're undeserving of their true dreams and desires. They feel embarrassed and guilty about having big dreams, yet they also worry that their goals are too simple, and that they're being stupid to expect success.

This affects their business because whichever way they turn is stressful, so every step triggers a fear that they will fail, fail and fail again. This reinforces the feeling of failure and limitation and the endless cycle of never feeling good enough.

Help your Achiever client by shedding light on why they feel undeserving. Unearth the reasons, clear them, and programme in a new story that they're worthy of success, however they choose to achieve it.

The impact of this work on their business will be increasing clarity around their true path, and a deepening level of self-appreciation for who they are, and what they are capable of. Their increasing self worth will serve them in all aspects of their business.

THE STRATEGIST

The Strategist gets distracted from their purpose because they don't trust themselves. They're notorious for spending a lot of time asking advice, and then completely ignoring it and doing something else.

This affects their business because they constantly feel that they're on the wrong track, and they'll pick up and drop projects like hot potatoes, and they just don't know why they can't settle.

Help your Strategist clients by finding out why they feel the need to be constantly busy, as it's probably a way of distracting themselves from something painful that's also creating a lack of self-trust. Only do this if you have the tools to do so, because it's not fair to poke at an old wound if you're not equipped to heal it.

This will impact their business because they'll finally be able to get in touch with their purpose, and their massive ability to take action will be channelled in the right direction. This is immensely freeing for The Strategist, and may well be the greatest gift that you can give them.

THE HUSTLER

The Hustler gets distracted from their purpose because they're so busy maintaining their suit of armour. Outwardly, they've got it all figured out. Inwardly, they are vulnerable and spend a lot of time thinking about everything. This prevents them from tuning in to the next evolution of their purpose.

This affects their business because they're often expending so much energy controlling their emotions and marching down a path with great determination that they miss out on connecting to their true mission.

Help your Hustler clients by allowing them to feel their pain, and creating a safe arena for their anger, shame and guilt to be released. The sooner you get them to love themselves, the easier they'll find it to concentrate on their purpose, rather than being distracted by putting a mask over their self-hate, self-anger and self-disappointment.

If you gain the trust of The Hustler and you're capable of helping them connect with deeper layers of truth, you have the potential to really help them leap forward. When these clients are aligned with their purpose they're powerful change-creators who spark magic for themselves and those around them.

THE GUARDIAN

The Guardian gets distracted from their purpose by impatience and desperation. Their unwavering faith in the power of enthusiasm means that when results don't come quickly, they start to doubt themselves, or they get discouraged or bored. Then they start to feel stagnant, and this triggers frustration, fear and desperation.

This affects their business because when desperation gets mixed in with the eagerness these clients feel to convey a message, it makes their communications frantic and desperate. As anyone who's been heartbroken knows, that's not a sexy combination.

Help your Guardian clients by finding the beliefs and fears at the root of their need for immediate gratification, and release them. Sort out their self-doubt, because it triggers all their feelings of not being good enough or worthy enough, and their progress starts to crumble like the little pig's straw house.

Doing this work will impact their business because without desperation and self-doubt spoiling the party, you'll be able to help them find the synergy between all the skills that they have and all the things that they enjoy. If you can find that common thread and help them to make it work in a way that feels good to them, they'll strike gold.

THE THINKER

The Thinker gets distracted from their purpose because they don't think they can make money using their gifts. They're often keeping their 'magic powers' hidden.

This impacts their business because they might be making money, but they have an underlying dissatisfaction with themselves and their lives. They have big dreams and desires, often involving travel, and they're pulled away from their purpose by focusing on being 'practical'.

Help your Thinker clients to trust themselves, and remove their limiting beliefs that they can't create wealth by following their passion. Clear all the old patterns and behaviours, because if you trigger their uncertainty, they'll be out of that superhero suit and back into their work clothes before you can say Bat Phone.

This work is immensely freeing for these clients, and they'll begin to see that all of their skills and gifts are valuable, and that creating opportunities, finding love and traveling in the way they dream of can be the result of doing the things that they love to do.

THE LIGHT

The Light gets distracted from their purpose because they don't recognise how wise they are. They're here to light up the world with their message and their wisdom. The problem is they're waiting for someone to stamp them with an official "You Are Enough" before they can do it.

This affects their business because they keep paying for classes, courses and coaches, seeking the external validation that will finally mean they are qualified to share their message. Until they recognise their own gifts, it's unlikely that they'll be financially rewarded for having them.

Find and release the limiting beliefs, fears and past experiences that have made them doubt themselves, and clear the associated pain from their energy system. Work on their fear of rejection, and clear the stress they have around being called a fraud, and the fears they have around being successful and not being prepared for it.

This will impact their business because The Light often associates success with great risk – they fear a whole range of negative consequences, including the loss of loved ones, and even physical attacks. You must help them feel that it's their time and that they are prepared, and that it's safe to shine, because the ripple effect from helping them to light up is infinite.

⬭⬭⬭⬭⬭

When your client concentrates on their purpose, they feel fantastic. Even hard times are bearable, and hard work feels good, when it's part of their purpose. It's essential that you help your clients get clear about their purpose AND that you help them stay focused on it!

Wealthology Money Block:

SELF-DISAPPROVAL

auren was so used to being hard on herself that she didn't recognise which voice was hers and which were those of her parents, ex-boyfriends, and old teachers. She sucked in disapproval and bundled it together until it began to choke her progress. Think of a cat with a hairball in its throat. Or don't, it's not the most pleasant image. But you get the point – if we don't have clear systems to deal with criticisms, over time they become harmful, and we can't function properly. Lauren was constantly talking badly to and about herself, and a lot of the time she didn't even realise she was doing it. Her business, relationships and health were all suffering. She was lost, confused, frustrated and miserable.

Lauren had put in 18 months of dedicated mindset work, focusing on her self-talk, forcing herself to be kind, journaling, affirmations, self-care, tapping; everything she could think of to try and release the negative thought-loops that her brain-train rode around on. Yet nothing seemed to make a difference for more than a few days, and it was a constant battle between her and her thoughts. Every time she wrote something for her website, or posted on social media, the voices got louder and the self-doubt and self-disapproval made it almost physically painful to continue. Unsurprisingly, her business failed to get off the ground.

Lauren came to see me at the end of her tether, frustrated and embarrassed about her lack of progress after a year and a half of dedicated self-work and trying to build a business. With muscle testing, we identified that Lauren's self-disapproval had taken on a life of its own, and was causing all sorts of problems and triggers that were making it impossible for her to make progress.

Lauren doubted herself, and then disapproved of herself for doubting herself, which made the self-doubt more severe. Every time she took action to move her business forward, it created more reasons to criticise herself. She also had some issues with not allowing herself peace, so any time she felt relaxed or that she was enjoying her work, it triggered a feeling that she was being lazy, and the self-disapproval kicked in again. We also found a similar cycle with her self worth – she attributed any setback to her low self worth, which she then beat herself up for, which lowered it further.

We worked on some other issues, with self-disapproval being the key block. Within weeks of her final session, Lauren went on to completely change the focus of her business, and is fully connected to her purpose. She's currently lighting up Facebook with authentic, well-received posts about her mission, building a strong following, and launching an online course that she's proud to talk about.

Here's what she said…

"Everything is positive. I actually have self-belief now, and a feeling of 'I deserve it' has really kicked in. So many exciting things are happening, I feel great. Shame and embarrassment were holding me back so much last year. I can't believe how different I am now. Everything has changed."

Shall we find out how you can help your clients with self-disapproval?

THE ACHIEVER

The Achiever disapproves of themselves for not having enough expertise, not knowing more, and for making too many past mistakes. This blocks their progress because they don't believe they can be trusted, and they doubt themselves.

This makes them more susceptible to negatively comparing themselves to others, and stops them from sharing their ideas, thoughts and opinions, which is the backbone of any marketing strategy, especially in this modern age of the online entrepreneur.

Help your Achiever clients by breaking this cycle; otherwise they are going to struggle with success. Find the root cause of their need to be so hard on themselves and clear it. Identify the things they really dislike in themselves, and release them. Raise their self worth and clear their blocks to being kind to themselves.

Clearing up these negative thought patterns impacts their business because it means that The Achiever starts to feel good, and is able to take action and move forward consistently, which is a huge component to success in any endeavour.

THE STRATEGIST

The Strategist disapproves of themselves for not working fast enough, not getting immediate results, and not having all the answers. This need-for-speed slows down their process, because every second they're not achieving high standards and rapid results they think that they're failing.

Their business suffers because they jump on their own ideas like a rabid dog on a bone, tearing it to pieces until they're exhausted and frustrated. Ironically, you could give them the same idea and ask them to put it into action for their own client, and they'd immediately see it was possible, and set the wheels in motion.

Help your Strategist clients to break this cycle of self-torment, or they will always find running their own business a struggle. You can ask them, or muscle test to quickly find the exact reason why they don't believe they deserve as much patience and space as other people. Release the blocks, so that they can slow down and stop whipping themselves.

This impacts their business because it restores a huge amount of their power. They're able to nurture their own ideas, trust themselves, and really take considered action on the things that feel good. This creates a new, upward cycle of self-approval, and gives them the ability to celebrate their wins, which encourages more self-belief and leads them to greater success.

THE HUSTLER

Hustler clients disapprove of themselves for being weak, feeling wounded, and thinking about past hurts. This blocks their progress because they don't give themselves space or permission to heal, so their business decisions are often governed by old pain that they're in denial about.

This is frequently the biggest thing holding The Hustler back – they are often aware of the unique gift and skill that they bring to the world, and know what their business is and how they want to run it – there just seems to be some mysterious reason that it never quite soars in the way they wish it would.

As well as healing the old pain, you must help your Hustler clients to release the idea that pain is weakness, and help them to forgive themselves for being wounded. If you don't do that, then the next time the client is hurt or if another old wound gets triggered, disapproval will kick in again and it will affect their ability to create and enjoy success.

Doing this work and breaking them out of the pain-disapproval-pain cycle can be transformational for The Hustler and their business. They'll begin to make clearer, aligned decisions and things will really start to take off.

THE GUARDIAN

The Guardian disapproves of themselves for getting angry, feeling stressed and judging other people. This blocks their progress because although they're just being human, they think they're a terrible person, and therefore unworthy of success.

This impacts their business because it has a dramatic affect on their ability to talk positively about themselves or their work. Marketing is not an easy task when you find it extremely stressful to communicate how good you are, and they especially struggle in a business that bears their name or identity.

Help The Guardian by showing them that there's no shame in being human, and help them to release their painful inner-disapproval about things they are angry about. Unlink the energetic connection between 'negative' emotions and worthiness of success.

Replacing their self-disapproval with self-acceptance can create enormous change for Guardian clients, as it really gives them the ability to show up right now, just as they are, rather than hiding out until they feel worthy of success, at some mythical time in the future.

THE THINKER

The Thinker disapproves of themselves for being foolish, for feeling discouraged, and for not working hard enough. This blocks their progress because the inner-voice of disapproval drowns out their intuition, higher self and inner-knowing of their true calling.

This impacts their business because it makes it really hard for them to get onto the right track and create a business that feels aligned. They get more discouraged, so their self-disapproval increases, and the cycle continues until they're essentially paralysed and can't see a way forward.

Help your Thinker clients to break this cycle by releasing the stress around the idea that 'feeling discouraged is failing'. Release the beliefs that they are foolish, and not working hard enough.

Clearing up these old thought patterns will impact their business because it means they'll be able to move forward, in alignment. More than ever, the modern entrepreneur wants to feel aligned – if you can help The Thinker to achieve that, they'll be forever grateful.

THE LIGHT

The Light disapproves of themselves for not knowing better, for dreaming too big, and for having stupid ideas. This blocks their progress because they are so hard on themselves that they shut down and play small.

This affects their business because it's difficult to create success – and really enjoy it – when you take your best ideas and body-slam them to the ground because they're 'too big'. These clients will have plentiful examples of times they have held back their truth, silenced themselves, and not put a plan into action because their inner critic was so loud.

Help your Light clients to realise that the world literally needs them to dream big and explore their ideas, and that they shouldn't 'know better' because a lot of the time they're doing things that have never been done before. Release their fear of looking stupid, and help them clear their subconscious of the fear of other people's disapproval.

The impact on their business is that their big ideas can finally be birthed into the world, and when that happens, these stars can truly shine. They'll be able to keep making progress, expanding, and glowing brighter, and as this is how The Light attracts money and creates wealth, things will really start to take off for them.

⬤⬤⬤⬤

Don't let your clients struggle with negative thought patterns. It's so unnecessary. Smashing the self-disapproval blocks is easy when you have the right tools, and doing so creates enormous leaps in your client's progress.

Wealthology Money Block:

HIGHER SELF

Before we get into this, let's clarify what the higher self is, because it's a bit of an abstract concept until you understand it in energy terms.

It's not your soul.

It's not your spirit.

It's not some sort of God or higher power.

Think of the higher self like an energetic placenta. It sits between the outer layer of your energy field and the 'Universe'. The higher self is the part of us that's connected to the Universal wisdom, and if we're connected to it, then we're dialled in to that wisdom.

Think of it as the part of your client that has a big-picture view of everything, and can therefore give them brilliant advice. That's why it's 'higher' – it has a bird's eye view. The more clear, connected and aligned your client's energy fields are, the more they receive information from their higher self.

Their higher self helps your clients in all sorts of ways, giving them information, ideas, and guidance on the best way forward. Helping them to access this wisdom is one of the greatest gifts you can give to a client, because it will keep serving them long after you stop working with each other.

That amazing $45,000 launch that changed my life? Seventeen percent of that success was because I was being guided by my higher self at every step. (I know that because I can muscle test to find out.) When launch strategists and online marketing experts have asked me about the numbers from that launch, they want to know… how many people were on your list? How many of them bought the product? How many Facebook ads did you run? Who was your launch manager?

I answer them – 46 people were on my list and I added 300 people in 48 hours. One hundred and twenty of them 'bought the product'. I didn't do Facebook adverts and I didn't have a launch manager. They can't understand it. The numbers don't make sense to them. I've given up trying to explain that they're asking the wrong questions. It's not about numbers. It's not about 'strategy'. It's about being in alignment with your purpose, being guided by your higher self, and being clear of all the blocks that this book talks about.

I have proved this theory a few times by ignoring my higher self and having some epic business fuck-ups. During my next launch, 8 weeks later, people started asking for refunds from my existing programme. That was unheard-of, and un-nerving. I muscle tested for the problem and it was 'Commitment and Indecision'. I realised that I'd switched off my higher self, been guided by money to create a new product that didn't inspire me, and the refund requests were a reflection of my lack of alignment and a sign I was out of integrity. I ended up cancelling the new product, refunding $3000 to the people who had signed up, and making a public apology. It would have been easier just to listen to my higher self in the first place. And saved a LOT of time and stress.

Oh, and then there's the time I forgot to listen to my higher self, and listened to others instead, taking their advice about how to write my copy and talk about my work, and it was very 'salesy' and tactical. Physical clue something was off: I felt ill, and even had a stomach-ache and a runny nose for two weeks. Financial clue: instead of welcoming the intended 150 new members to my group, 17 trickled in. If your client is blocking money, they're quite possibly blocking their higher self.

My last launch was $72k, and you can bet I was listening to my higher self the whole time. Put it this way, if you had an invisible 'friend' who could see the whole map AND the best route, waiting to help you navigate to your dreams, would you ignore them?

Exactly. So let's find out what's blocking your client from using their higher self…

THE ACHIEVER

Achievers block their higher self by believing that they are flawed, and therefore don't feel that it's safe to trust their instincts.

This affects their business because they're so disconnected from their higher self that instead of hearing an inner voice of support, they imagine the criticism that they will receive, and don't take action.

Work with your Achiever clients to improve their self-image, so that they love their flaws and accept their imperfections. Clear the stress around how they see themselves, then release the belief that it's not safe to trust their instincts.

Doing this will allow them to open up to their higher self; creating space for their spark, and inviting in optimism and hope. They'll gain a lot of clarity, begin to generate ideas that feel aligned, and take action that inspires them in a way they never have before.

THE STRATEGIST

The Strategist has a deep-seated belief that no one helps them, and as the higher self is a source of help and guidance, it remains completely blocked. They feel that they have to be so independent, that they even shut down their internal voice of encouragement.

This affects their business because they don't realise that this unique 'higher' wisdom is one of the keys to unlocking the authenticity they seek, and so they struggle to consistently connect with their audience.

Help your Strategist clients by releasing their blocks related to the belief that no one can help them. This will help to clear the connection to their higher self, and it will stop them attracting advice from people who can't help them.

The impact on their business of reconnecting their higher self will open up a whole new support system, and give them the gift of authenticity that's often missing in their business connections. This can be an absolute game-changer for your Strategist clients.

THE HUSTLER

The Hustler blocks their higher self by controlling their thoughts so strictly that they don't allow any space for the higher self to be heard. They are terrified of feeling the pain that might rise up if they stop focusing their thoughts on the road immediately ahead.

This affects their business because they stray from their true calling, and are distracted by things like money, and the demands of other people who need help. They'll often make rash decisions and rapidly change things in their business, without stopping to get totally clear on what they truly want.

Help your Hustler clients by encouraging them to be truly honest about what they want. You must release their fear that change is painful, and heal enough of their pain that they're able to open up completely.

The impact of this work can be truly inspirational. If you hold space for The Hustler to connect to their higher self and create an image of their dream business, and then shift their energy into alignment with it, you can step back and watch the magic unfold.

THE GUARDIAN

The Guardian blocks their higher self by having an almost chronic tendency to deny the reality of their situation, and as the higher self deals in truth, it's unable to communicate with them.

This makes it hard for them to confidently move forward in their business. Instead of getting constant divine downloads about which direction to take, they have to rely solely on their mind, which makes them feel anxious and awkward.

Work with your Guardian clients to help them accept the reality of their situation. This can be a big job and you must tread carefully and be absolutely sure of your abilities. Don't open the client up to the pain of their present if you are not sure that you can help them to heal it and deal with it.

This impacts their business because allowing The Guardian to be more conscious of the truth creates a connection with the higher self, and the wonderful wisdom that resides there can be a new source of empowerment, courage and divine guidance.

THE THINKER

The Thinker blocks their higher self by denying their true ambitions, and because the higher self tries to communicate their purpose, they completely shut it down.

This affects their business because they think they have to have all the answers mapped out in front of them before they're able to change anything. The think this is a sign that they'll fail, so they find it very hard to get started.

Work with your Thinker clients to clear the belief that they have to have all the answers, and release the stress around admitting that they have ambitions to do other things, even if they don't know what those things are.

This will impact their business because the higher self will then be able to guide them to make great connections, and they'll begin to attract people and opportunities that make them feel included, loved and supported, and everything will begin to move forward.

THE LIGHT

The Light blocks their higher self by refusing to be honest about their superpowers, and as the higher self is a form of superpower, it's completely closed down.

This means that their real essence, their essential truth, remains hidden, and their business doesn't reach the great heights that it would if they would step fully into their magnificence. In marketing, they resist the pull to just share, and light up, and just go for it.

Work with your Light clients to open up to their complete self, so that they can see and experience the fullness of their gifts. Clear their resistance to their superpowers. Release their fear of discipline and fear of speaking up, so that they can express themselves without fear of consequence.

The impact on their business from this work will be profound. Clearing the blocks to the higher self will mean that it can begin guiding The Light to share their message in a way that is aligned with their true self, and not the half-self they present to the world out of fear.

◯◯◯◯◯

Although this Wealthology theme might seem light-weight or abstract, this work is essential. Please don't under-estimate the power of a healthy higher self-connection when it comes to helping your clients to create wealth!

Wealthology Money Block:

CONTROLLING

We all control. It's human nature. Even the most easy-going amongst us like to have a certain amount of control over some things. It shows up in all sorts of places and it's a hard habit to break. It's probably something you hear clients joke about — 'I'm such a control freak.' Do you really know how much their need to control blocks their success? Let me tell you: way more than they realise.

When your client is trying to control an outcome, they will only move as far forward as they can whilst still feeling in control. They'll subconsciously keep their circle of influence small. They won't market themselves and put themselves 'out there' because they can't control what the outcome will be. Control is an illusion, and it's one that your clients cling to, because it gives them a sense of safety. Work through their control issues and help them to get into the flow of life – genuinely. There's a big difference between flowing with the river and being dragged along by it, panicking and trying to grab over-hanging branches.

How do you completely let go and take your stressed controlling energy out of the business? And genuinely out, not in a 'I'm going through the motions of doing something else but my head is still at my laptop'. (I've done that too.) The answer for me is energy work. Muscle testing for the blocks that are stopping me from loosening my grip, and then releasing them with a couple of Energy Edits. Every time I do that, doors open and money flows in – and most importantly, I'm able to step up to the next phase of evolution in my business, and take the leaps forward that I was scared of before.

I confess that sharing my secrets in this book, and teaching my block-smashing methods at the Energy Editing practitioner training, would not have happened without me eliminating some pretty big control blocks! These included fear of not being needed, of making myself obsolete, of having my work stolen, and of having someone train with me and then abuse their powers. Doing the inner work has meant that my 'outer work' looks vastly different than it did last year, and I'm now using my gifts in ways that allow more people to experience them on a deeper level. I'm creating more wealth for myself and my family than ever before, and it all feels good. When we deal with our control issues, life is exciting and exhilarating without being stressful.

Your clients subconsciously know that a big step up in their business means the outcomes are unknown, and that terrifies them, so most often they don't make the leap. Releasing the need for control enables them to jump up, even though they don't know exactly where they'll land.

Each Wealthology Profile has a different way that control shows up in their life, different reasons they hang on to it, and different blocks that it causes. If you can help them clear those blocks, they will begin to enjoy more synchronicity and serendipity, and they'll also be able to take much healthier risks, step into the next phase of their evolution, and enjoy the wealth and success that comes with it.

Let's look at where to focus your skills for each type of client...

THE ACHIEVER

The Achiever controls their desires. They see everything that they want, and deep down they think that they can't have it until they're rich, or thin, or better in some way, so they control their desire to have it.

This affects their business because they stop putting energy into making things happen, and subconsciously self-sabotage any progress they do make. No wonder they don't achieve their goals!

Help your Achiever clients by showing them the pattern. If you dig under this, they often have a hidden belief that if they had really wanted something, it would have happened. They often won't have shared this with anyone, so it's become a festering shame-scar, stopping them from moving forward.

Clearing their control blocks will open up a whole new way of thinking, feeling and behaving for The Achiever, which allows them to start creating a foundation for the business that they truly desire.

THE STRATEGIST

The Strategist controls their pain. They're often tense, stressed, and anxious, and they will not want you to know that, because then you would know that they aren't in control.

Putting on a brave face blocks their ability to authentically connect. This affects their business because their need to be sure of outcomes even means that when they attempt an 'authentic, vulnerable share', it can come across as carefully-managed and disingenuous.

Help your Strategist clients by holding a space where they can relax enough to be vulnerable. You must be trustworthy. Clear the blocks that keep them afraid of being authentic. Whose approval are they seeking? Why are they so worried about letting their guard down? Make sure you have the proper tools to release and heal these blocks before you start digging.

Releasing The Strategist from their need to control how they are perceived has a great impact on their business because it allows them to be truly authentic, including in their relationship with themselves. This results in much greater client-attraction powers, and allows them to relax into enjoying their work.

THE HUSTLER

The Hustler controls their actions. They manage their behaviour in order to avoid any situation where others might become hostile towards them, because they find it very distressing when people are angry with them.

This need to self-protect is a huge barrier to success. They either play it safe and don't go all-out in their business – or they go all-out and find it extremely stressful and begin to self-sabotage.

Helping your Hustler clients release the fears that underpin their need to control is essential. If you can, use muscle testing to find the exact fears; there are generally two or three that are the foundation for this 'house of terror', and when you release those, everything shifts and they'll stop holding back.

When The Hustler isn't held back by worrying about criticism, anger and hostility, they will really begin to step up and shine. They'll reach larger audiences, connect with the people who need to hear their message, and their potential client base will grow exponentially.

THE GUARDIAN

The Guardian controls their behaviour. They put limits on themselves, so that they're not 'inappropriate'. They constantly try to adapt to their circumstances and make sure everyone else is ok.

This has a dramatic effect on their ability to succeed. They'll often come very close to creating the business of their dreams, and then sabotage it or stop taking action, so that they don't upset or offend those around them.

Help your Guardian clients by releasing the belief that their natural behaviour is inappropriate. Clear the stress around the idea of being a maverick, and remove the fear that being unique and different isn't safe for them. Find out why they are so worried about other people feeling uncomfortable, and help them to expand their view of what is 'appropriate'.

When you help The Guardian to release their need to control their own behaviour, they will begin to see how wonderful they are, how much they have to share, and how much pleasure others get from the sharing. They can enjoy the fullness of their own spirit, without feeling the need to apologise for it, and can soar in the way that they are meant to.

THE THINKER

The Thinker controls how they are seen. They think that if their true nature were revealed, they would be judged and no longer included.

This means that they often go over the top with people pleasing, and are over-kind and over-concerned, usually at the cost of their own time and energy.

This has a profound effect on their success, because they keep themselves invisible, by holding the focus firmly on everyone else's talents, needs and wants. These clients often think that it's the people around them that don't notice their skills and powers, but truthfully, they hide their own super-powers, out of fear they will no longer be part of the 'tribe'.

Help your Thinker clients to release their fear of not being included, so that they can begin to focus on their own path. Then help them to release the need to control other people's focus, so that it's not so stressful for them to be the centre of attention. Clear the past pain around being ostracised, and trying to keep quiet and blend in.

Without these blocks in their way, they can easily explore their gifts and how they want to use them, and everything else will begin to fall into place. Helping The Thinker to bring their light out into the open is a great honour. It serves them and it serves the world, because the ripple effect of their work is often huge.

THE LIGHT

The Light controls their brightness. They often have a deep-seated belief that if they shine their light as bright as they can, then everything will be so successful, so fast, that they'll leave their loved ones behind.

The cost of holding this belief is an unconscious limiting of everything that they are capable of, and it has a dramatic effect on their success. They will sabotage by not following up on opportunities, and being half-hearted about the next steps towards their goals

Help your Light clients with this because it's often a key block to their success. Identify the root of the beliefs, fears and past experiences and clear them. Release their need to limit their brightness and visibility.

If you can do this work, everything starts to change. The Light starts to truly radiate brilliance, and their highest potential explodes into a whole new realm of possibility and wealth, which they can fully embrace without self-sabotaging.

○○○○○

Releasing your clients' need for control will not only allow them to step into the next phase of the business evolution, it will make them much happier, calmer and more content. What's not to love about that?

Wealthology Money Block:

SELF-PUNISHMENT

Your clients are punishing themselves. A lot. Most of the time without realising that they're doing it, and certainly with little understanding of why or how to stop doing it.

Enter you. Break these patterns and you'll help your clients create massive breakthroughs.

Robert came to me completely exhausted, burnt out and working punishing hours to cope with his growing business.

I muscle tested to find out what was going on, and found that the problem was being manifested inside his energy system. This was interesting, as it wasn't a block in the energy, it was a behaviour – the energy system was actually creating a problem, by replaying old beliefs that there was a problem.

We dived into the work and I found that Robert had a history of feeling dejected and defeated. When I told him that those two words had come up in my muscle testing, he gave me a tired smile and said 'You just described my whole life Michelle.' We quickly released the stress and past pain related to those emotions using an Energy Edit.

The next part of the work was around the concept of Robert needing to be dependable, and being stressed by his past experiences of not being dependable. He was carrying a lot of old hurt, and giving himself a really hard time for some mistakes that he'd made when he was younger. He was self-punishing by working long hours, pushing himself hard, and feeling guilty if he stopped. We gently released the stress, along with the anger he was carrying. Finally, we moved on to a powerful Energy Edit for 'Forgiving myself' and as that processed, a great sense of peace fell around him.

He was tired after the session, and I gave him my standard self-care protocol to help the work process without any detox reactions. When we next spoke he was like a different person. He said he felt completely different, he was no longer 'acting out' at the people around him, he was enjoying his work far more, had more energy, and was so much happier that his wife had noticed, and when I met her she confirmed this and thanked me. Able to see that he deserves happiness and success, Robert began to capitalise on his hard work, his income amplified, and he's now creating a successful career as a speaker, traveling internationally to speak at high-profile business events.

That's why you need to know why and how your clients are self-punishing. Are you ready to find out?

THE ACHIEVER

The Achiever punishes themselves because they subconsciously believe that there has to be struggle and sacrifice to achieve their goals – it can't be easy, and there has to be a problem.

They hold back from success, because if it's perceived to have come too easily then they fear they'll get lots of attention, and people will be jealous. They don't know how to cope with jealousy, so they punish themselves by self-sabotaging so that they don't risk punishment from others.

Work with your Achiever clients so that they recognise what's going on. You must help them to integrate the belief that it's safe to stop punishing themselves, and that it's not dangerous for them to be successful. You also need to release their fear of jealousy, and retribution from others. Demonstrate to them what self-love looks like, and raise their self worth so that they become more comfortable with showing themselves kindness.

The results of doing this work will be obvious in their business. They'll be able to encourage themselves to act without sabotaging all their efforts before, or immediately afterwards. They'll also be much more willing to be visible. The Achiever's life – and your job – will be a lot easier when they stop punishing themselves.

THE STRATEGIST

The Strategist punishes themselves because they subconsciously believe that they are weak. They worry about letting people down, and they hold back from asking for the sale, or 'closing' the client, because their worst fear is having a conversation about something they did wrong.

This impacts their business, because to avoid that scenario, they self-punish by sabotaging opportunities. They have lots of great ideas, and even generate a lot of leads, and a lot of goodwill, and then fail to convert it into revenue. Every time they want to serve at a higher level, they stumble back into these old habits, and it costs them a lot of time and money.

Work with your Strategist clients to release their fear of letting people down. They will have buried painful past experiences, where they feel that they've failed. Don't crack open this can of worms unless you have the tools in place to truly help. Help them to process these perceived transgressions and to forgive themselves. Then you can build their confidence, inner strength and faith in themselves.

This will have a fantastic impact on the business because they'll be comfortable having essential conversations about money. This is often a transformation The Strategist is expecting from their coach – get it done!

THE HUSTLER

The Hustler self-punishes because they have a subconscious belief that it keeps them safe. It's a form of self-protection; if you're punishing yourself, you're more prepared when you come under attack. They self-punish by second-guessing themselves constantly, and running mind-movies of all the ways they can get things wrong.

They can't project their true big vision for the future because they're so busy preparing for adversity in the present. They work crazy hours, find it hard to switch off, and don't allow themselves to see the truth of their full potential, which massively impacts their enjoyment of their business, and means they fail to capitalise on the money they could make.

Work with your Hustler clients by releasing their need to constantly beat themselves up, and programme in alternate ways of thinking.

Remember that you're talking about removing the way they keep themselves safe – you need to know what you're doing, and don't set this as homework because they won't be able to do it themselves. When you've done the work, clear the belief that self-punishing protects them from potential negative outcomes.

There is deep work to be done with The Hustler here, and it will transform their entire way of life, as well as their business. Suddenly, they are open to their true potential, and can see a much bigger vision for their life's mission. Harness this vision and their new feeling of inner peace to their innate determination and watch this client fly.

THE GUARDIAN

The Guardian punishes themselves because they have a subconscious belief that it protects them from being disappointed. They stop their own momentum, and avoid flying too high, so that they don't have too far to fall. There's an element of 'getting in there first' before someone else lets them down.

They always hold something of themselves back, and take teeny-tiny steps towards their goals, instead of the enormous strides they are capable of. You'll also find evidence of this in their marketing; look at the About Me page on their website and it's unlikely to be a story of self-celebration that excites their audience and incites action.

Work with your Guardian clients to heal their wounds from past disappointments. If you can't do this, suggest they seek support from someone qualified to do so. It's important and essential work. Clear their beliefs that they can't risk disappointment. Help them to forgive themselves and others. Work with them to build their courage, and change how they think and speak about themselves.

When you give The Guardian wings, and teach them how to get off the ground, magic happens. This might be one of the most rewarding journeys you will support a client on. Having healed the past, released the fear of disappointment, and buoyed with fresh courage and your support, the results will be evident in everything from their personal relationships to their bank balance.

THE THINKER

The Thinker punishes themselves because they subconsciously believe that it creates security. It keeps them in a mind-set of lack and fear, which they think is what stops them over-spending and making financial mistakes.

This means they get very stressed about money, time and energy, when it comes to themselves. So they hurry through life, busying themselves with everything and everyone else, and their focus is fragmented, so they get easily frustrated. This makes building a business really difficult and has a drastic affect on their growth.

Work with your Thinker clients to release the belief that they must self-punish to keep themselves secure. Help them work out a new system for measuring security, and map out alternative ways to 'protect the treasure' so that they realise that they're inherently responsible beings, and they're not going to start wildly wasting money if they start being kind to themselves.

If you help The Thinker to slow down enough, it creates space for ideas to rush in, which will help them to wake up to their gifts. One of the things they need to wake up their dormant superpower is rest, so they need to release their beliefs around self-punishment keeping them secure. Be the catalyst for this change.

THE LIGHT

The Light punishes themselves because they have a subconscious belief that it keeps them small enough to avoid being punished by others. They self-punish by really letting the negative self-talk go into overdrive.

They expend a huge amount of time and energy blaming themselves for things that haven't even happened, and worrying about what people will say about them. It has a huge impact on their business, because they're not only holding themselves back from taking needle-moving action, they're also creating a huge amount of negative energy around their work!

Help your Light clients by showing them that they don't need to punish themselves. As you do this work they will often have a deep realisation that most of what they perceive as punishment is coming from within themselves. You must release the negative thought patterns, and the quickest way to doing that is removing them from the energy system.

This work creates a profound shift towards shining their light instead of beating it down. The double impact of suddenly feeling able to speak up and boldly move forward, coupled with no longer creating a cloud of negativity around every action they feel courageous enough to take, is huge! Stop The Light from self-punishing, then stand back and see what happens – you will both be amazed.

⬤⬤⬤⬤⬤

Self-punishment behaviours have a nasty habit of kicking in at opportune moments, and making these changes will serve your client in a million ways. When it comes to their ability to make money, this essential work is the sort of valuable transformation clients will come to you for.

Wealthology Money Block:

ANGER

Anger blocks your client's energy system in a number of ways. Some clients bottle it up, some bubble over with it, some avoid it at all costs, and some steep in it most of the time. Some clients have no idea they are angry, some are carrying anger so old they don't know it's there. They might be holding on to anger they saw a parent demonstrate, or being affected by a societal anger that's so second nature to them they don't realise it's even an issue to be addressed.

Whatever the cause, when anger is present and not processed, it causes problems. It might be that there is an obvious relationship between anger and their ability to make money. More often, there are symptoms in their income, and no obvious indication that anger is a cause. That's why you need to seek out where the unprocessed anger is, identify what it is, and release it. Do not poke the bear if you don't have tools to effectively support this process – it's not fair to the client to 'have a go' at helping them with anger issues, and raking up old pain that you can't release - you must know what you are doing. If you can't do it, suggest they seek appropriate support.

Georgia came to me when she was in the middle of launching a group programme and was finding it hard to talk about money when it got to that part of the conversation. She was totally confident in asking the right questions, and confident in the value of the programme, but when it came to sharing the price, she felt stressed and wasn't signing up members at the rate she had anticipated.

I muscle tested and identified the issue as 'Underlying anxiety that money will run out'. Further investigation found that seeing her parents argue over money when she was young had led to a subconscious belief that talking about money leads to anger and tension. We did some quick Energy Edits to release the belief, and also to release the past pain of feeling worried and tense when her parents argued. There was also a self worth issue from being bullied when she was eight years old, so we released the fear of getting hurt and the feelings of anger around bullying, to unblock her energy and raise her self worth.

We worked for one hour, and two weeks later Georgia reported back to me that she had "absolutely no tension whatsoever around talking about money, and my closing rate has gone up 30% - no joke, massive difference!" To put that into tangible numbers, for every ten people Georgia speaks to about her $2000 programme, she now makes an extra $6000, on top of what she'd already been achieving. No joke indeed.

You probably have clients just like Georgia, who have everything going for them, and when it comes to the money conversation, they choke. Maybe unprocessed stress around anger is their money block and smashing it will change everything.

Here's what you need to know…

THE ACHIEVER

The Achiever gets blocked by anger because every negative experience they have takes on a life of its own, and creates an angry story that gets stuck in their subconscious. Each single 'stuck story' replays itself, growing in detail and distortion from the facts, and they meld and blend into one another.

Their inner stories about not being successful are so charged with angry energy that any new stories of potential are quickly drowned out. The tiniest thing can quickly activate the negative feelings and shut down their momentum, which creates a painful cycle of self-sabotage and false starts.

To truly help The Achiever, you must work through this issue, or recommend someone who can help. They need to realise how much anger they are carrying, to accept that it's safe to let go of it, and then to release it. Then comes forgiveness, for themselves and others. Help them take responsibility for their own actions, without slipping into self-blame.

When The Achiever releases anger, they begin to truly feel joy. This emotion may have eluded them for a long time. These clients will suddenly be able to recognise their own achievements and feel that they are worth celebrating. They're suddenly able to get ideas past the initial stages without it feeling impossibly hard, and their business gains real momentum, perhaps for the first time.

THE STRATEGIST

The Strategist bottles up their anger, out of fear they'll return to a past pain, or be like an angry person that they know. Anger represents instability and insecurity to them, and they work hard to keep it locked down. It then manifests in a constant feeling of stress, which threatens to bubble up, and they think that something is wrong with them.

In business, they keep choosing clients who are hard to work with, and they expect criticism, so feel constantly uneasy. They seem to repeat their mistakes, because they're often attracted to familiar paths, with similar people. They don't realise that they're being led to the same feelings of pain because there is something to be healed.

Help your Strategist clients to identify the painful situation from the past, which keeps repeating itself in the present. Muscle testing is by far the most effective way of doing this, as you can get straight to the root cause without having to churn up all the painful memories to find the one you need to clear. When you've found the old pain, release it, acknowledge the lesson within, and heal the wound, both emotionally and energetically, to prevent the pattern repeating.

When The Strategist releases anger, they're able to let go of the familiarity of working with critical and difficult clients. They'll no longer fear that serving at a higher level, and raising their prices, will mean more stress and blame. They'll feel a great sense of relief, and experience the emotional freedom to grow their business in a way that serves them too.

THE HUSTLER

The Hustler feels that they aren't truly seen by others. Deep down, they're furious about this, and they don't realise it. This manifests as a deep drive to prove who they are, and to show those who don't see them that they're worthy of being seen.

This impacts their business because they direct their compass towards money, status, and material gains, and begin to feel very lost, often spending increasing amounts of time on their own. Struggling to navigate their emotions, their anger increases and they either jack in the business completely, or manifest problems that affect their income.

Work with your Hustler clients to acknowledge their pain around their real self not being seen. Then release the anger about that and allow it to process. Heal the emotional and energetic scarring that comes from not feeling seen as they really are, often over their whole lifetime. Help them to reconcile the truth of who they are and firstly, to see it themselves!

Doing this work can be a shift from night to day for The Hustler. They connect to their true self, and stop feeling they have to prove themselves. Greater opportunities manifest, they find their flow, and because they truly see themselves, others can see them too. Their marketing stops being something they do, and becomes an extension of who they are.

THE GUARDIAN

The Guardian thinks showing anger will lead to isolation. They don't think it's dignified to show that they're angry and will go to great lengths to make excuses for other people's behaviour, rather than allow themselves to clearly communicate that they're not happy.

They will stay in business agreements that don't serve them, undercharge for their services, and essentially sacrifice themselves to avoid confrontation. They are so good at tuning into other people's needs that it amazes them that they should have to explain that they're frustrated, as to them it should be obvious.

Work with your Guardian clients to show them that it's ok to be angry, that there is always a way to hold boundaries with dignity, and they are fully entitled to their own feelings. Clear the relevant beliefs, and release the fear that they will be isolated if they speak up for themselves. Hold space for them to really be themselves, and to express their frustrations.

This process can be very empowering for The Guardian, and it's very much a part of them stepping into their own best self, to realise they can be completely themselves, anger-and-all, and be very much loved and respected for it. Doing this work will pay dividends in their business. Everything will start to shift, and they'll enter new partnerships and opportunities feeling able to set boundaries and uphold them.

THE THINKER

The Thinker gets blocked by anger because they've wandered off their spiritual path, and aren't making their personal evolution a high enough priority. They become short-tempered, and their usual gentle nature can be quite abrasive.

The affect on their business depends on how long they ignore the signs that something is wrong. The longer they ignore their calling, the angrier they become. Sometimes they aren't aware that they're tense and high strung. The tension feeds their fears and unhelpful thought patterns, and they can become very stuck, in a job or business that they don't enjoy.

The Thinker clients like to forge their own way, so you must hold space for them to make their own realisations and discoveries about how anger shows up for them. Help them to forgive themselves for being angry, and to release the tension and stress they're carrying. Release the belief that they need to limit themselves, and connect them to their inner power, because that's truly the only way to stop the anger and break the cycle.

Supporting The Thinker through this exciting time is a real gift. When they get aligned with their highest path, the anger and negativity start to drop away, and their life will move forward in wonderful ways. Income will start to flow in from unexpected places, and will be a monetary confirmation that they're on the right track. They'll also begin to trust their intuition, which will guide them to greater opportunities.

THE LIGHT

The Light has a tendency to see obstacles as insurmountable. When they see a mountain, they think they have to climb it, rather than flow around it, so they spend a lot of time frustrated, or angry that they're just not good enough.

This really slows progress in their business, because rather than hitting a challenge and knowing immediately that they can overcome it, they first enter a spiral of beating themselves up for not having all the answers. Sometimes the obstacle seems so hard to pass, that they freeze, or start moving backwards. This makes them feel fragile, and incapable, which makes them angrier, and so the cycle continues.

Work with your Light clients to show them that they are capable of finding simple solutions to complicated problems. Help them to release their anger and old pain around not feeling good enough. Healing these wounds is essential, because it enables them to see that they are competent and can make things happen quickly.

The impact on their business can be quite something! Imagine The Light suddenly knowing that there is a solution to everything? Removing this block can literally mean that they get into a flow-state where everything starts to move forward and amazing things start to happen.

Being able to smash the money blocks related to anger is revolutionary work, and means your clients get great results, which means your business is successful. If you don't have the tools to safely, gently and quickly help people with their hidden pain, please refer your clients to someone who can assist them.

Wealthology Money Block:
ENCOURAGEMENT

The origin of the word 'encourage' is found in ancient French, meaning to 'make strong'. It comes from the words 'en' – to put in – and 'corage' – courage. To put in courage, and make strong… no wonder encouragement is a huge source of power and progress for your clients, and such a fundamental part of this book.

It should be simple; encouragement feels good to give and receive, we get and gift plenty of it, and we're filled with courage and made strong, and we race towards our dreams in complete alignment.

Sadly, it's not quite that straightforward, and in reality we all have a block around encouragement that activates triggers, flicks us out of alignment, or kicks us off our path.

Happily, you're about to learn what these blocks look like, and how to sort them out.

Emily came to me very stressed because she'd lost four clients in quick succession. Without warning, $7000 in monthly income had disappeared, and she still had to pay all her outgoings. Emily knew that the losses were an indication something was going on with her energy, and felt there was an invisible limit on what she was allowing herself to earn.

I muscle tested and found that there was a subconscious income cap, and to smash it we needed to work on 'self worth and past experiences of being discouraged'.

Emily had many experiences of being discouraged as a child, and painful memories of being eager and excited, and then told off and punished. There was a big block in her energy system that was triggered when things got 'too exciting'. The pain and the related block were released in a few minutes with an Energy Edit.

We did more work around feeling defeated, and the stress that she'd subconsciously associated with feeling encouraged, and we integrated the ability to receive understanding in a way that feels good. We also cleared the belief that she was disobedient, and released her pain around authority figures.

Two weeks later, Emily reported that she'd experienced a massive shift in her relationship with money. She'd easily replaced the four clients, which was $7000 per month, and was excited about some new ideas. With the stress around 'excitement' gone from her energy, she was able to put these ideas into action, and within a few weeks had generated another $2000 monthly on-going income. That's an additional $9000 per month, just from one session of Energy Editing. She'd also run a hugely successful event, established her reputation and increased her credibility with her target audience, and was excited about calls she had scheduled with the next influx of clients.

That's what happens when you clear the blocks around encouragement. Shall we...?

THE ACHIEVER

The Achiever gets blocked by encouragement because they need it so much. They even say 'I need encouragement'. They want to feel that they're doing well, and without encouragement they find it hard to take action. They have huge amounts of self-doubt and will constantly check in with other people before and during decision-making.

Their business is affected because they rely on other people's input, opinions and cheerleading rather than listening to their intuition and making the best decisions for themselves.

Work with your Achiever clients to help them see that the only person whose encouragement really matters is their own! Release their need for constant support from other people and light the inner-spark of self worth that will ignite their ability to encourage themselves. Clear their resistance to connecting to their intuition.

This will reap great rewards. The Achiever will become increasingly able to make decisions for themselves in tune with their higher self, and for their own life purpose. They'll stop people pleasing, and the encouragement of others will be a bonus to celebrate, rather than a required component before anything can get done. Their confidence will start to gain momentum, and so will their business.

THE STRATEGIST

The Strategist allows encouragement to interfere with their original ideas and plans. They have an idea, and seek out other people for encouragement. Too often, what happens is that the feedback comes in the form of opinions and changes to the original idea, and they lose sight of what they wanted to do, and it no longer seems appealing.

This affects their business because for every thousand ideas they have maybe one will come to light. It deflates their confidence, and makes them increasingly reliant on other people because they lose their ability to trust themselves.

Work with your Strategist clients to build their confidence and release their attachment to needing encouragement from other people. To do this you'll first need to clear any past stress related to seeking approval from someone who they desperately wanted to impress. This can be emotional work, so make sure you know what you're doing.

This will have a great affect on their business because they'll finally be able to do the things they really want to do. Their income will increasingly come from the people and places they truly enjoy serving, rather than things they have to do to make money. Rather than having a hundred exciting ideas and trashing them whilst they continue to do work they don't want to do, they'll begin to take action on them. This will be a huge breakthrough.

THE HUSTLER

The Hustler is determined not to need encouragement. They're so used to being independent, and ready for criticism, that they go full-force into their new ideas impulsively, with their guard up.

They're so convinced they mustn't allow themselves to be encouraged, that they act impulsively, with a false sense of courage, and this affects their business. They miss out on the wisdom that others have to offer, and the guidance that would lead them to a much easier, more abundant path.

Hustler clients like to go it alone, so if you've been given the privilege of being their coach, it's not a role to take lightly. They will expect to move forward fast and will be very quick to say 'screw this, I'll do it myself.' Work with your Hustler clients to release their old pain around having ideas criticised. Clear their blocks to encouragement, so that they can allow it, listen to it, and believe it when they receive it.

This will be like a dark cloud lifting off their business. The Hustler who allows in encouragement becomes even more successful, and finds so much more joy in their work. They can get into flow, align with their purpose, and create wealth in a way that lights them up. Encouragement is a huge piece of the puzzle for these clients, and when you help them slot it into place, they will become your biggest cheerleader.

THE GUARDIAN

The Guardian focuses so much on encouraging other people that they forget to encourage themselves. They're subconsciously expecting everyone else to show up and cheerlead for them in the way they do for others, and when this doesn't happen, they assume they're not loved, because to them, loving someone means encouraging everything about them.

This has a detrimental affect on their business, because they get an idea, and put their own excited fuel into getting it off the ground. Then they wait for others to come along and help the idea to take flight, and when it doesn't happen they get very disappointed, assume the idea is bad, and that no-one cares, and their own excitement is killed off.

Work with your Guardian clients to find out why they don't feel that they're worthy of their own encouragement. The fastest way to get to the core belief here is to muscle test for it, because it's probably something hidden under a load of old stories that you'll have to dig under. Then help them to release the pain of disappointment over all the times they have felt let down when others haven't shown up for them. Help them to clear any blocks that prevent them from speaking up and clearly asking for support.

If you get this piece nailed down, their business will reap the rewards. The Guardian who isn't solely reliant on the support of others is a powerful force for good. They will find everything easier when they're more aware of the dynamics of what they need, and how other people behave when it comes to encouragement. This understanding of their own character, and the ability to ask for what they need, can be a game-changer for these clients.

THE THINKER

The Thinker gets blocked by encouragement because they've usually never had enough of it. They just don't know what it feels like to be encouraged to follow their path, think of themselves, and do what they really want to do. They're often carrying a huge amount of pain from past experiences of not having their true self encouraged.

They feel trapped by other people's expectations, and the thought of going against the grain, or doing something different, is terrifying. Their view of what's possible for them is extremely limited, and they feel boxed in, but don't know how to break free. Their confidence is usually damaged or non-existent, so it's not only hard for them to conceive an idea, but almost impossible for them to move forward assuredly with it.

Work with your Thinker clients to release the pain from not being encouraged in the past. It's a massive trigger in their system and is holding them back from doing anything that seems remotely 'risky' in their business. Identify and clear the fears and doubts that are keeping them trapped. Clear up the negative thought patterns related to why they're not worthy of encouragement, and programme in the belief that they can encourage themselves, and that it's safe to do so.

Doing this work will open up The Thinker to all the options that are available to them, and giving them more confidence to take action. Breaking these clients free of all their old limitations around other people's expectations will pay dividends, and they'll begin to move in new directions, and re-ignite old passions. What a gift to give them!

THE LIGHT

The Light feels that encouragement has to be deserved. They apply this rule to everyone, especially themselves. They make constant, subconscious judgements about who should be encouraged, and only praise when their invisible requirements are met.

They rarely meet their own high expectations. Instead of spreading joy and encouragement, they withhold it, which blocks the flow of positive energy around them and their business. They're constantly passing judgement on themselves: Do I like myself today? Am I worthy of praise? And the answer is often 'no', so they don't encourage themselves, and they don't move forward or rise up to serve at the next level.

Show your Light clients that it's time to release their feelings of unworthiness, so that they can see themselves as deserving of encouragement. Find and clear the cause of their belief that they're unworthy. Don't dig up every painful memory, muscle test for the root of the problem, the original, key incident, and clear that. Release their need to judge themselves and others.

Imagine a client with a wonderful message to share with the world, who keeps slipping out of alignment because they're constantly judging themselves, and deeming themselves unworthy of encouragement from within, and from others. Now imagine that client constantly encourages themselves, and is able to really accept praise from others, and stays in alignment a lot of the time. What do you think the difference in their business is going to be? And what do you think the knock-on affect in your business will be when you're the facilitator of this change for The Light? Huge. For all involved.

⚬⚬⚬⚬⚬

Other coaches aren't looking at 'encouragement' in this way, because people don't realise it's a huge area when it comes to money blocks. You now know exactly what to look for, and what to do about it. Awesome. Let's keep going…

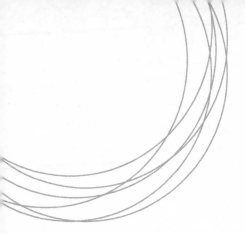

Wealthology Money Block:

SELF-ACTUALISATION

'm skipping the part where I share all the meanings that have been given to this term since its conception by Kurt Goldstein in 1934. (I had to Google that. Thanks Wikipedia.)

In this work, for your clients, it means they know that they can be what they want to be. It refers to having the ability to know that they can fulfil their true potential, exactly as they want to. This is important because generally your clients will only do what they believe they can do. When you remove the blocks to self-actualisation, you open the client up to knowing that they can be what they want to be. This can be a truly remarkable change.

Harry came to me for help because he knew he wasn't fulfilling his potential. Despite being a published author with a following who celebrated his work, his own method for helping people that got powerful results, and corporate clients who liked hiring him, he wasn't making enough money to support himself and his wife, and he was ready for that to change.

The first thing I found was a belief that 'being eager about making money for myself is disgusting'. After we released the belief, Harry told me that in the past he made a lot of money for charities, and found it a lot easier than making money for himself. We then released the stress around the idea that 'empowering myself must lead to generosity'. Harry said that every time he thought about making money, he automatically started thinking about how he could give it away. During the Energy Edit, he had a profound realisation that 'Empowering myself IS generosity. I love being on stage and people always tell me that they're really inspired when I speak.' Harry began to see that generosity takes many forms, and that his need to be generous didn't have to mean giving away everything he earned. If you're subconsciously deciding you have to give all your money away, it's eventually easier for your subconscious to make sure you don't earn it in the first place.

Next I found a belief that 'money has to be made from hard work, otherwise something will go wrong', and an accompanying fear 'of things happening to me beyond my control'. Harry told me that this was one of his biggest fears, it showed up frequently in a recurring dream, and it was a big trigger for him. He didn't realise that, combined with his accompanying belief that bad things happen if you don't work hard, it was blocking him from being able to truly step into his passion for being on stage, because he found that easy and joyful. His subconscious put these two together and concluded that following his bliss, and becoming all he wanted to be, was dangerous.

He also worried that his love for comedy and ability to make people laugh was 'not a real gift' and that it was about him showing off. I identified a deep fear; 'petrified of liberation' and after doing the Energy Edit, Harry shared that 'it was all about disappointing my Dad.

It started as what people think, and then it all traced back to my dad, and not wanting him to think I'm a goof.' A final Edit on 'my life's work' and Harry released a huge amount of stress, and came out with a clear vision that: 'I have to put fun first. That's who I am. Leading with ME can resonate into the business world.'

I told Harry that my testing showed he would feel profoundly different in six days. True enough, within a week he called me a 'superhero' and reported that he'd secured his two highest paying consecutive days of work EVER, for corporate clients who were going to be served by a self-actualised, funny, Harry. Lucky them.

Self-actualisation: Knowing that you can be all that you want to be.

It's a game-changer, and honestly, it's really fantastic for your business when your clients call you a super-hero.

Ready?

THE ACHIEVER

The Achiever thinks they're too flawed to share their real selves with the world. They're often burdened with 'secrets' – resentments, feelings of being undeserving, and negativity – that they think they have to be pure of before they can become what they want to be.

This affects their business because they feel that self-actualisation is to be perfect, and they're searching within and without for a magic key to unlock the box where the perfect them is hidden, so that they can hold it up for the world to see, and step into their full potential.

Work with The Achiever by releasing the stress around all the hidden parts of themselves that they think make them unqualified to make money as the person they are right now. Also, help them to be authentic without feeling the need to share their entire past. They can share what feels good to share, what they think will help the people they want to help, and that which is aligned with their purpose and message.

The affect on their business will be a huge feeling of relief, as they realise that their 'secrets' are not a reason to not have the business and life that they want. They'll realise that the person they are right now 'can be what they want to be'. That's the key here. It doesn't open a magic box; it opens up The Achiever to see themselves in this moment, as perfect in their imperfections, and someone who has something important to share. It's a beautiful transformation to see, and will impact all sorts of people, in all sorts of ways.

THE STRATEGIST

The Strategist evades self-actualisation because they don't want to go through the discomfort that comes just before change. They do everything to avoid feeling their own growing pains. When they feel challenged, they look for external reasons, and avoid feeling their own pain in the way they need to for change to occur.

This affects their business, as they remain unfulfilled and doing work that doesn't truly excite them, simply because they won't sit in their discomfort long enough to transform. They spend years in a job they don't like, and maybe transition to serving clients who stress them out, because they fight self-actualisation.

Work with your Strategist clients to identify the pain that they're avoiding. Don't do this if you don't have the right tools. You mustn't irritate wounds that you are not capable of healing; it's just not fair to your client. Release their fear of this pain, as well as the pain itself. Hold space for them to shift into the transformation on the other side of the displeasure. This is literally like protecting a rare caterpillar whilst it struggles to emerge as the butterfly it's intended to be.

The affect in their business can be just as wonderful as the rare butterfly. Indeed, it is rare that The Strategist will find their way to being what they want to be, unless they do this work. A self-actualised Strategist is a powerful being, because when their nature and work ethic is applied to doing what they actually want to do, magic happens.

THE HUSTLER

The Hustler gets blocked from self-actualisation because they think they're listening to their intuition, when it's actually the voice of fear. They believe they're being guided to success, and keep trusting their gut feelings. What they don't realise is that they're not actually depending on their intuition; they're listening to the fears that are trapped in their subconscious.

This obviously impacts their business, because when they're faced with a dilemma or a big decision, they often turn where their fear directs them. If they were aware of these fears, they'd refuse to let them run the show, but these fears are well hidden – they're the master puppeteers of The Hustler's life, and they haven't written self-actualisation in to the show.

Find the deep fears that are blocking them from knowing they can be what they want to be. If you can muscle test effectively, that's the best way to get to the absolute truth of the matter. Release the fears so that they're no longer responsible for making big decisions. Check for anything else that's blocking the intuition and clear it, then help your client to recognise the difference between a gut feeling of fear and a gut feeling of intuition.

This will be an eye-opening process for The Hustler. It's like taking off a really heavy, wet coat that they had no idea they were wearing, and feeling the sun on their skin for the first time. They will usually assume that their income, if they become self-actualised, will have to drop from where it is currently. This doesn't have to be the case if you combine energy work with a decent business plan to map out the best way forward.

THE GUARDIAN

The Guardian thinks no one will be there to help them when they become what they want to be. They worry that they're going to rise up, and then crash back down because they won't have the help they need. They don't want to achieve their dreams, to immediately see them slip away.

This affects their business because they keep delaying, waiting for a mysterious time in the future, when they have enough backing and assistance from others, before they self-actualise. They can be what they want to be, but not yet. Often they're sitting on a dynamite idea that will blast them to their dream destination, and they just don't feel prepared to light the fuse.

Work with The Guardian to release the beliefs that their dream will be a lot of work, and that no one will support them. Clear their fears of doing everything alone, and release past pain around being unsupported. This especially affects the solo entrepreneur who doesn't have a team around them, so it's an important block to look out for. Bring them back into the present, and help to increase their faith that the perfect people and the perfect path will be there for them as they move towards their dreams. Assist them in putting a plan in place to make this happen.

The affect on the business will mean they realise that they can be what they want to be, now! They can see the path ahead clearly and are ready to get moving down it, and if that future has a team in it, they can start building it, without waiting for it to be complete before they self-actualise. This can be a game-changer for The Guardian.

THE THINKER

The Thinker can't self-actualise because they don't feel free to express their uniqueness. They can't imagine a time, or place, or group where they would be accepted if they became what they wanted to be.

This affects their business because their message, gift and special talents stay completely undiscovered, or kept secret, or talked about so quietly that there is no danger of shattering the illusion of belonging. This makes marketing a real challenge! It's hard to attract clients when you can only whisper about what you do, to the few people who already know you.

Help your Thinker clients to release the stress they have around the idea of expressing their own uniqueness. The thought of it will probably make their eyes widen in fear. Clear the fear of what happens when you don't conform. Release the pain of all past betrayals, and the sadness that goes along with it. Help them to process the hurt of their past experiences, and to come to a place of peace with their past.

Doing this work will enable them to feel it's possible to be what they want to be – probably for the first time in their lives. Once The Thinker has this feeling, things will start to shift and change, and serendipities will occur as they step into the idea of claiming their power and start doing the things they really want to do. They'll begin to realise there's actually a demand for the 'weird' stuff that they've been afraid to share.

THE LIGHT

The Light thinks self-actualisation will mean that their friends no longer like them. Connection is extremely important to them for a sense of peace and security, and they fear that they'll be ejected from the tribe if they become what they want to be.

This affects their business because they hold back from up-levelling and going for their true goals. They have no idea how much their subconscious is sabotaging their dreams, by conjuring up images of isolation, and backstabbing, and being gossiped about. It has a massive impact on their income, and is often one of the biggest factors when their revenue has plateaued.

Work with The Light to identify and release the exact fears they have around this issue. Remember, the subconscious is fed by the energy system, so you need to find the problem and clear it from there, otherwise it will re-occur in the future. Look for blocked thought patterns around being criticised, and release old pain related to being mocked, talked about, and left out. They will probably have been through a change in friendships before and found it very stressful. Release the stress, blocks and energetic misalignments related to that, so they can begin to truly self-actualise into the next phase of themselves.

The impact on their business when you clear these blocks is far-reaching. When The Light suddenly feels that they can be what they want to be, they become a powerful being! This issue has often been a major cause of their invisible income limit, and removing it means they can begin to rise off the plateau and enjoy more money flowing in.

⬤⬤⬤⬤⬤

Self-actualisation is an essential part of the individual's evolution; in fact, it's the whole point of life! This is an integral part of the work you will do with every client, and when you have a reputation for helping people step fully into what they are intended for, you won't find it difficult to grow your own business.

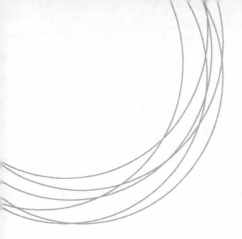

Wealthology Money Block:

ABUNDANCE

Everyone's talking about clearing blocks *to* abundance. But what about the blocks that are caused *by* abundance? Yes, it's a thing. These are the fears, doubts and triggers that are activated when things are going well. When things are good, these blocks kick-start the subconscious into thinking 'it's too good, we don't know if this is safe, we want familiarity'. Even if familiarity was rubbish in comparison to this new, abundant state, the mind will find a way to sabotage and get you back there.

Even with a healthy awareness of these invisible restrictions, they slow down progress immeasurably. Being able to identify the exact beliefs, fears and blocks at the core of the problem, and then quickly release them from the energy system, is the quickest way to smash these limits and get your client soaring.

Patrick had a big vision for his business, and when we worked together he had a great idea that was in its infancy. He told me that his biggest current challenge was sustaining momentum, in order to bring more clients on board.

As we moved through the session, muscle testing revealed that Patrick's subconscious had linked the idea of great wealth with running a large organisation. Patrick consciously was very aware that he didn't want a complicated business model; and he did want a hugely successful business. This meant that every time he started gaining momentum, the abundance was triggering the subconscious to slow things down, out of a misplaced fear that it would turn him into a workhorse. We untangled those two concepts in his energy, so that his subconscious would stop holding him back from creating more wealth when things started moving forward. Patrick said that during this Energy Edit he could feel the burden of that imaginary business extinguishing his spark, and at the end the weight lifted off him completely, and he felt free to light up, and bask in abundance.

Ten weeks later, Patrick messaged me: "I believe in you and your work, and I've definitely experienced shifts from your magic… I had a $250,000 month this month." And this was on the 23rd, with one week to go! Can you imagine how that feels, when you help someone and they make a quarter of a million dollars in a few weeks?

I'm guessing you're ready to clear up your clients' blocks that are caused by abundance.

Here's how…

THE ACHIEVER

The Achiever gets triggered by abundance because they don't think they can have it all. Their automatic reaction to gaining in one area is that loss in another area is inevitable. This scarcity thinking plagues them; it rears its head and spoils their joy and growth, by pulling them back down to familiar levels, both emotional and financial. This is self-sabotage on steroids.

This affects their business because when they gain something, perhaps an opportunity to work with someone they admire, they immediately assume something is going to go wrong. They fear they'll mess it up, or create a disappointment - or that if it does go well, that there'll be consequences in another area of their life. So they don't seize the opportunity and make excuses, or go for it, but only half-heartedly, so that it doesn't happen.

Work with your Achiever clients to release the beliefs and fears related to 'having it all'. It's a lack-mindset that will keep tearing them down every time they make progress, unless you get to the bottom of it and get it cleared. They often have problems with not trying their best, and not going full-out at every opportunity, because they are scared of the consequences of both succeeding AND failing. This is the ultimate rock and hard place – sort it out for them so they can accelerate towards the success they deserve!

Doing this will stop The Achiever's income being governed by self-sabotaging thoughts. Right now their subconscious fears are running the show, and they're not able to serve at a higher level or move towards their big dreams. Changing this can transform everything – suddenly they're able to see opportunities, seize them, and actually enjoy them! This is essential work, because these patterns will keep repeating, and freedom from them is a true gift that will serve your client for a long time to come.

THE STRATEGIST

The Strategist gets blocked by abundance because it makes them stop communicating honestly. They think it means they have to be in a state of perfect bliss and gratitude at every moment, and able to take care of everything and everyone. They avoid having open dialogue, and allow their boundaries to be crushed.

This is especially true when they get a client investing at a higher level; they feel abundant, and for a time, everything is good. Then their client might start adding extra tasks and expectations to the original agreement. The Strategist, in a state of abundance, finds it very hard to have the necessary conversation to re-establish boundaries and clarify the arrangement that was made. Instead they begin to resent the client, they no longer enjoy the work, and they lose their sense of abundance. They will then subconsciously sabotage other potential clients from coming on board to avoid the situation happening again.

Work with your Strategist clients to find the hidden causes and reasons why they can't communicate honestly when they're feeling abundant. There will often be a particular memory or experience that is the cornerstone for this entire tower of beliefs and fears. I strongly suggest muscle testing for it rather than asking them to consciously bring up all their old pain. As always, don't do this unless you have the tools to completely clear the hurt and heal the emotional and energetic wounds.

The impact on their income will often be quite dramatic. Without realising it, they will probably have been resisting creating new clients out of fear of repeating this old pattern. They'll be able to look with fresh eyes at their business, and decide what they really want to do, and how different things can be now that they're able to communicate honestly – particularly with the clients who invest at a level that makes them feel abundant! Can you imagine what a difference it makes to these clients to no longer feel shut down when they're paid well? This is important work!

THE HUSTLER

The Hustler struggles with abundance because it inhibits their ability to be themselves. They start to think that being abundant means they have to look, act and behave a certain way. They will upgrade everything from homes and holidays to handbags, because they believe that's what abundance looks like, and they often create a situation where they feel trapped by higher outgoings in a lifestyle they don't know how to change.

This affects their business because they're not operating as themselves, and they become increasingly unhappy. They often find themselves doing work they don't really want to do, in order to sustain a lifestyle they don't really want to live. They don't know how to get out of it, because the abundance is blocking their ability to be themselves, so the pattern continues. They also often assume that if they were to change tracks, that they'd lose the abundance they've created, so they don't want to entertain the conversation. This really is a cycle that self-perpetuates.

Work with your Hustler clients to release their beliefs and stuck thoughts around what abundance means, and what it looks like. Dig deep for the stories that they're telling themselves about money – there are usually one or two that are keeping them stuck in this position, you need to find them and clear them completely from the subconscious and the energy system, otherwise this pattern will keep recurring. Also clear any beliefs around how they can only make enough money doing the work that they're currently doing.

The impact of this work can be huge, as you'll enable them to open up to the truth of who they really are, what is the life they really want to live, and what do they really want to do. They'll no longer be carrying around a heavy bag of self-expectation to do things out of a misplaced belief that abundance looks a certain way. The Hustler will then be able to really look at what is valuable to them, in all senses of the word, and to take action to make their true dreams a reality.

THE GUARDIAN

The Guardian doesn't think they're worthy of abundance. When it shows up, all their feelings of low self-worth are activated, and they start to question if they deserve it, which quickly spirals into a fear that they will lose it. They almost visibly shrink in size, and make themselves small, so that no one notices them, because they subconsciously believe that if anyone realised they had this abundance, somehow it would be taken away.

This impacts their business because they'll only attract abundance for things they don't mind losing. Corporate job; that's ok to be paid well for. Client they don't really like; that's ok too. Big dream that they would love to have success with? No chance! They can't risk creating any wealth in that, because someone might see that they aren't worthy, and take it away. This is one of the key reasons why they'll repeatedly come close to something they really want, or do it as a hobby; they're always flying just below the radar to avoid detection and destruction.

Work with your Guardian clients to raise their self worth by carefully clearing the past pain and shame that makes them feel unworthy. Help them to see themselves as complete, and deserving of abundance. Hold space for them to step fully into their biggest vision of themselves, and to remain 'big' within the vision, and release the emotional triggers that cause them to shrink back and halt their growth, so that they can keep expanding, creating and receiving.

This is essential work and The Guardian will benefit from doing it. When they're in a pattern of expansion and contraction, they make much slower progress, because they're always conscious of not rising too high or being too big, and losing everything. Without this pattern in place, they can really enjoy the abundance that they attract, and fully appreciate it, and in that state of appreciation, worthiness, and joy, they'll create more abundance – and this becomes their upward cycle rather than a downward spiral.

THE THINKER

The Thinker gets blocked by abundance because it makes them feel guilty. When things get easy and begin to flow, they have a tendency to feel apologetic, and think they should be focusing on other people. They shift their focus away from their own plans and desires, and give all their attention to anyone else who asks for it. They feel that they can't say no because they feel blessed in their own lives. This then flips them out of flow, and reduces their natural state of joy, which benefits no one. They are the classic example of running around trying to fill everyone else's cup from a pot that is half empty.

This affects their business because they never dedicate enough time to themselves, for what they really need and want to get done, so everything suffers, from personal self love and care to things they need to do to grow their business, like writing copy or talking to clients. Eventually when they feel bad enough, they'll give their own desires some attention, and things improve, they get into flow, and then what happens? Those abundance buttons get pushed, the guilt kicks in, and they're back to running around after everyone else.

Work with your Thinker clients to release their guilt. Find out why they feel bad for other people when they're in a state of abundance, and clear the beliefs and fears related to it. Just like a river needs banks to protect its ability to give life, these clients need boundaries, so that they can fill their own cup, in order to fill others.

The impact on their business will be profound. The Thinker usually thinks they're a procrastinator when it comes to building their own dreams. That's not really the case. What's usually going on is that it's so hard for them to find the energy, time and resources to focus on their own work, and doing so makes them feel guilty. Changing this can change everything. Suddenly they're able to drive their own drive, on the path they want to take, because they're not involved in everyone else's journey.

THE LIGHT

The Light assumes that abundance means they have to do more. They forget that their success is linked to their ability to 'be' rather than 'do', and revert to over-production mode, in a misguided attempt to maintain the wealth. They equate their rising value to working harder, and think that in order to keep creating abundance they need to keep creating 'stuff'.

This affects their business because instead of relaxing into the feeling of abundance and allowing it to magnify in easy ways, guided by their intuition, they just get busy. Working extra hours, throwing out ideas, over-complicating things and just generally making life hard for themselves. They get bogged down in details and lose sight of the ease and grace they wanted to enjoy. Suddenly a simple idea has an intricate, time-sucking, energy-vacuuming, ten-step email funnel that they need to create all the content for, and they're working in the middle of the night, and beating themselves up that they can't afford to hire someone to do it for them.

Help your Light clients by clearing this workhorse mindset from their belief system. Find the related fears and thought patterns, gather them all up, and torch them. Bring them back to their true value, and help them to see their intrinsic ability to create wealth just by being who they are and sharing their message in simple ways that feel good. Clear their stressful ideas around what being rich and successful looks like, and release their need to limit themselves with old-fashioned beliefs about what creates abundance.

The affect on their business? You'll practically be able to see their website breathe a sigh of relief, as they let go of all their workhorse triggers and allow themselves to settle into creating abundance and enjoying the process of seeing it appreciate. They'll remain connected to their intuition far more easily, rather than disconnecting when they get a new idea or an influx of money. They begin to really relax into creating abundance in ways that seem easy and fun, and have a real sense of claiming their whole, brilliant self.

⬤⬤⬤⬤⬤

Looking for the blocks caused by abundance keeps your clients moving forward. Without doing this work, they'll take more time to make less money, and they'll keep hitting income plateaus. Get it done and they'll continue to create the wealth they deserve.

Wealthology Money Block:

SELF-LIBERATION

This chapter is about the liberation that comes when your client knows they can think what they want to think. Most clients – and coaches - don't realise that there's a distinction between this and self-actualisation. They think that when they decide to be what they want, and step into their big vision for themselves, to talk about their mission or their brand and to really be it, that the work is done. They're then surprised to find that everything still feels like an uphill battle, and that they're still hustling and pushing. Where's the ease and grace they expected? Why is it still hard to make money? The answer is this: they still don't own their thoughts. Externally they've changed, and are standing up to lead, and they've often done a lot of self-development to get to that place. Internally, they're still conforming. They have no idea that on a subconscious level, they don't have freedom of thought.

For your clients, self-liberation is the internal state that accompanies the knowledge that they can think what they want to think. It isn't just saying what they think. It's knowing that they are entitled to think whatever they want. It means that they're comfortable with having their own ideas, and sharing them in an open forum. It means they develop their own theories and opinions about things. This is the work that creates thought leaders. It is true freedom, and no matter what level your client's business is at, when they master this, they'll see a huge leap in income and a massive reduction in stress.

After my first $45,000 launch in 2014, I went on to have a great year in my business, working with clients in packages with an investment one hundred times greater than in the practice I had closed down before I cleared my money blocks. In June 2015, I could sense that the flow I had been feeling was slowing down, and I was in a 'busy' mind-set. Things weren't feeling fun and exciting. Something was going on with my energy, and therefore with my subconscious, which was altering my thoughts, which were affecting my behaviour.

I started muscle testing. I found a belief, and a corresponding fear, that worrying about money was keeping me safe. It made me feel in control. I feared that if I didn't worry about money, that it would all disappear, and that I'd fail my family, and that I'd be made an example of, for having big ideas about money and money blocks. I was carrying all sorts of stress around authority, being punished for not fitting in, and for doing things differently. I had a belief that 'being different is dangerous' and my intuition was being blocked because I feared that the ideas coming in would make life unsafe.

I did the work to clear the fears, thoughts, beliefs and emotions, and felt an enormous sense of relief. Something had shifted. Shortly afterwards, I was thinking about money and energy, as I began to plan for the re-launch of my group programme in July. I knew that I'd used a different energy for the original launch than I did for the online course I'd created a few months later. Both had been easy, exciting, and successful, with the second one generating $28,000 – not bad for a couple of weeks of working two hours a day, enjoying myself and being in charge of the children for the school holidays, whilst Pete went skiing with a friend.

I started thinking and muscle testing about types of energies, and how they attract money. The energy I'd used for the $28k launch was different – I'd used targets, I'd had a plan, and I had a clear intention for the money I made. I knew that wasn't my natural state, it wasn't how I usually do things. Suddenly everything began to flow, I was receiving idea after idea, muscle testing and drawing on my experience with clients to develop the concepts, and before I knew it, I had a complete description of the six Wealthology Profiles, and how they make – and block – money. I didn't know what I was going to do with the information; I did know it was original, exciting, and the start of something new.

I had liberated myself from worrying about what other people might think about my thoughts and ideas around money. I no longer feared that I was going to get 'into trouble' or be slammed by some mythical authority figure for developing my own concepts and sharing them. Those 'profiles' became a quiz on my website, and people were reading their reports and emailing and messaging to tell me that they recognised themselves immediately, and found the information really useful. Their feedback confirmed what I had suspected – I had opened up a whole new way of looking at money and energy that could really help people. I decided to incorporate it into the programme I was about to re-launch. Prosperity Prescription 2.0 would have profile-specific work as part of the Energy Editing done for the members. The launch was a fascinating roller-coaster, and I was my own experiment; every time things slowed down, or I was holding back, I'd muscle test for what was going on, clear the block, and get moving again. Two weeks later, I'd welcomed over 100 members into my online family, and generated $72,000.

It didn't end there. The members loved the profile-specific work, and the results were so powerful, that I decided to make the entire programme profile-specific. As I started to think about this – because I was free to think whatever I wanted to think – something new started to take shape. I had a wealth of knowledge and experience of what blocks people from success and money, and I knew that particular themes came up repeatedly, and that many of my concepts were original. Before I knew it, I had the Wealthology Themes in front of me.

My confidence grew so much that when I was asked what I could teach in a two-day intensive, I didn't hesitate to reply: I can teach my method for working with clients to identify and smash their exact blocks to money and success. It immediately began to take shape. I ran my first in-person practitioner training in March 2016, and it was a true highlight of my life so far. It gave the trainees a hugely valuable skill, enabling them to massively expand their income potential, as well as giving them the ability to clear their own money blocks. This combination is what makes Energy Editing so powerful in growing a business. Just four weeks later, at the time of writing this, the certified Energy Editing Professionals are getting fantastic testimonials, signing up new clients, and raising their rates.

Back home, after six months of collating my research, and taking clients of each Wealthology Profile through my process, I was ready to write. The book you hold in your hands, the practitioner training that feels like my heart has found its home, and an ever-increasing income, is what happened for me and my business when I experienced self liberation. Imagine what will happen for your business when you can do this for your clients...

THE ACHIEVER

The Achiever struggles with self-liberation because they don't see the big picture for their business. They're so busy worrying about other people, and minute logistics, and micro-managing a million things that they don't connect to their mission. There's just no space for thinking about broader concepts or developing expansive ideas, so they block the possibility that they can think what they want.

They know what they want to create money for, and often have quite a skill for visualising what they desire: freedom, choice, travel, adventure. They also know how to hustle and get busy. They completely miss the part where they figure out what they believe in, what's important to them, and what they really like thinking about. They go straight from dream-life, to minute-business-details, which means they can end up wandering aimlessly, without a sense of what they're committed to or what they believe in.

Help The Achiever by finding out what's behind their attachment to the details. It will be a collection of beliefs, fears, thoughts and emotions; identify them and clear them. Do some work around their tendency to operate with false courage – they put on a brave face, stand up, shout something out to their audience, and then panic and go back into hiding. This is often because they don't know what their driving force is, so they lack staying-power and consistency. Clear their pain and embarrassment related to past experiences of missing details and acting with false courage. Finally, help them to connect to their mission and figure out what they're committed to.

When you liberate the thoughts of The Achiever, everything changes. They're suddenly connected to their mission, and can see a vision for their business, not just their personal life. And as entrepreneurs, business is personal! Giving them the freedom to think what they want to think opens them up to feeling truly courageous, perhaps for the first time in their life. They become committed, they know what they want to say, and they stand up and say it. That's true liberation: a precious gift that's yours to give when you can do this work.

THE STRATEGIST

The Strategist can't self-liberate because they don't honour their own creativity. They get the initial spark of an idea, and then stamp the life out of it before it can ignite into the flame it had the potential to be. They then become convinced that their ideas are bad, and therefore they mustn't think what they want to think, so the next spark automatically gets stamped on too. This becomes a problematic cycle, because the way they deal with their lack of self-liberation reduces the likelihood that they'll experience it.

This affects their business because they don't allow their ideas to flourish, and they doubt themselves, and the energy of that spreads like rot into everything – their marketing, their ability to sign clients, and ultimately, their happiness. What begins as questioning the validity of their own ideas, leads to them questioning everything, and this can be a time of great sadness and struggle for The Strategist that has serious consequences for their income.

Work with these clients to breathe life into their ideas. Find the root cause of their need to dampen their own creativity, and clear the related blocks. They often fear that liberating themselves would hurt other people, so they become caged within their own limitations. Release those fears and related beliefs and thoughts. Then locate the reasons for their damaged confidence; identify the original cause of them losing certainty in their own abilities, and clear the blocks.

When The Strategist is self-liberated, it can have a massive impact on their life and business. They begin to regain faith in their own ideas, and the increased confidence that comes from seeing their own creativity actually result in something, sweeps through into everything: the direction of their business, what they actually want to do, how they conduct themselves in conversations, their ability to talk about money. Realising that they can think what they want, and that they're entitled to their own ideas, beliefs and opinions, illuminates them in a way they've never experienced. This is essential work, isn't it amazing that you can do it?

THE HUSTLER

The Hustler fears that self-liberation will get them into trouble. It just doesn't feel safe for them to think what they want to think. They might have grown up around people who worried a lot about what others thought of them. They've often been punished for saying exactly what's on their mind, and this especially creates blocks when they know they are correct. They often have a huge subconscious fear of authority, or speaking out and being publicly condemned.

This affects their business because it cuts off their intuition, and limits their ability to connect to the big ideas that will explode their work to 'mission' status. It also knocks them out of flow, and keeps them in busy-mode. They continue to hustle, because they're not liberating the great thoughts and ideas that will easily generate the success they suspect is waiting for them. They will get to a certain level, and when the next phase involves a wider audience, their inner alarms are sounded and they block the 'dangerous' thoughts from coming through.

Work with The Hustler to find and clear the blocks related to their issues with speaking up and being punished. If you can do it precisely, identify their past experiences of being ashamed for something they did, and release the pain of getting into trouble with authority. Release their worries around thinking their own thoughts, and the fear of what would happen if they were completely liberated; it might be fear of failure, or public humiliation, or letting people down – and it could be all of those and more.

The Hustler will change immeasurably when this work is complete. They will stop feeling fragmented, and completely reconcile all parts of themselves – who they are, what they want to be, and of course, what they want to think. This self-liberation will result in a complete opening up to their own ideas, the ability to develop the work that they're meant to do, and to fully own and stand up for what they believe in. They'll connect to their true mission and goals, and be able to comfortably articulate what they are here to share with a wide audience.

THE GUARDIAN

The Guardian believes that self-liberation will cause dramatic changes that they won't be able to cope with. They have a subconscious belief that if they're suddenly free to think what they want, it will create startling transformation, with dire consequences. Their enthusiastic nature means that they automatically start to put a lot of energy into seeing all the things that can go wrong when these drastic life-changes occur.

This affects their business because it makes them reluctant to free up their minds and fully embrace the unique thoughts and ideas that are just waiting to be liberated, which keeps them stuck, and self-limiting. These clients are generally not living the life of their dreams, no matter how hard they try to convince themselves otherwise. The mind monkeys are having a secret party in the basement, causing chaos and trashing the place. Upstairs, all appears to be Pollyanna-perfect. In reality, they're crippled with fear that unleashing their true potential is just something they're not ready to cope with, and in turn, it makes their business suffer.

Work with your Guardian clients to get the mind monkeys out of the basement. Find out why they're frightened of change, and clear the fears. Release all the shady beliefs about them not being able to cope. This will be a lot easier if you've already done their self-actualisation work around being supported, however this is different; it isn't about other people, it's related to their confidence in their own ability to deal with dramatic change, especially in relation to success. Clear all the funky stuff they've got going on around what it will mean to truly become what they are meant to be.

The Guardian who can step up and own their thoughts, and be clear about what they stand for, is a powerful agent for change. Having resisted transformation themselves, they are able to really empathise and see the challenges other people have, and to hold space for others to make the same journey. The affect on their business is like a football manager realising she's been keeping all her star players on the bench to avoid them being injured. Suddenly, the big hitters are allowed out to play, and the whole game changes. Think of yourself as chief advisor to the manager; do this work and everybody wins.

THE THINKER

The Thinker doesn't self-liberate because they think too much. Ironically, they're unable to think what they want to think, because they're too busy over-thinking everything else. They are constantly bombarded by thoughts about the past, the future, other people, their own problems, and other people's problems. You name it, these clients probably think about it at least once a day. They just can't switch off the non-stop mind-chatter, and their brains are like a pinball machine, just pinging around to a million thoughts every minute.

This affects their business because they don't hit pause on the busy-thinking long enough for the good stuff to get any attention. Their purpose, their desires, their mission, their value, all of it gets drowned out. They feel stuck, trapped, and often get caught on a hamster wheel, wondering how they'll get off, and unable to connect to the answer, because they're too busy analysing a hundred other things that don't really matter. This continues until they're exhausted and drained, and totally fed up that they have no clue what to do about it.

Help your Thinker clients get off the hamster wheel in their mind. Find their attachment to over-thinking and free them from it. Clear their need to be constantly searching for solutions to tiny issues, and release the belief that they must be the answer to everyone's problems. Work with them to connect to the present moment, and help them figure out what entices them back into crazy-thought mode. Identify what distracts them from creating brain-space for themselves, and clear the blocks, so that they can be at peace with being at peace.

The affect on their business is profound. Instead of spending every waking (and many sleeping) moments worrying, analysing and stressing out, they begin to think clearly for the first time in a long time about what is best for them. Often that means they can spend periods without thinking at all. This is like pumping oxygen into their desires, and giving their dreams a chance at life. This is a real chance to help someone off the hamster wheel and give them much-needed freedom from their own methods of self-torture. These clients need you, and they will be sincerely grateful. This is a true liberation from the self, and the impact can be far-reaching, with a complete change in their trajectory.

THE LIGHT

The Light can't self-liberate because they don't think they're qualified to know what they know. They're subconsciously waiting for someone to give them an official stamp of approval before they feel entitled to think the thoughts they think. They look around at people with 'official' certifications, and compare themselves, and feel that their work isn't valid, and hold back from sharing it on a larger scale. The truth is that they usually have such a deep knowledge of their own subject, and such a unique message, that there is no one who can give them a diploma in it.

This affects their business because they hold back from doing things out of fear for the outcome. They don't trust themselves, and subconsciously expend a lot of energy worrying that a situation will arise where they don't know what to do. They tend to play it safe, and sabotage opportunities so that they remain at a level where they're comfortable that they know enough. They don't realise that they know so much more, if only they'd liberate their knowledge and allow themselves to think what they want to think.

Help your Light clients by releasing their resistance to being a path-maker. Find the beliefs that they aren't good enough, or qualified enough, or 'official' enough, and clear them. Do some work so that they can realise that they are perfectly acceptable, just as they are. Help them to accept themselves, because that is where acceptance begins. Identify what they fear will happen if they don't hold back, and release the fears and any related thoughts and beliefs.

This is the final piece in the puzzle that will allow The Light to turn up the power to their brilliance, and start really radiating their gift out into the world. Giving someone with an important message the permission they need to start sharing it is like giving an angel its wings.

Liberate these clients from the restrictions they've placed on their own thoughts, and experience the immense joy of watching them soar.

⬡⬡⬡⬡⬡

Self-liberation is true freedom. It eliminates most indecision and hesitation, and allows your clients to connect to their true mission, purpose, and desires – and then take action on them. If you're looking for the key to creating wealth from a place of complete alignment, make self-liberation part of your work.

MY WISH FOR YOU

L ouise was in the middle of launching a new high-ticket product, and was totally stuck.

This is her feedback after one money-block smashing session...

"Suddenly, a new purchase, then another, then a new client out of nowhere suddenly bought my highest ticket VIP coaching - the first ever! Everything freed up, money and perfect clients started flowing in. There has definitely been a profound shift in my life since the session. It's like the final restraint was removed, allowing me to really run my business. In the past fortnight I've had two major individuals contact me about collaboration, which would mean me working in Australia and America. It's extraordinary, exciting and I'm feeling no fear at all!"

And guess what?

I didn't do that session. One of my certified Energy Editing Professionals did it, using my method. She took the principles, added them to her coaching business, and immediately created that level of success for her clients.

When I asked her how it felt to get these results, she replied with an enormous smile:

"It's the ultimate icing on the cake! It's what makes my work worthwhile. I love what I do, and actually hearing from my clients the difference that smashing their money blocks has made to their lives, and seeing them free of their struggles, it just makes me beam! I'm so excited to keep exploring the potential of combined coaching and energy work, which will open up much deeper and profound shifts in my client's lives."

Isn't that brilliant?

That's what I wish for you.

Take this knowledge, apply it, and smash the hell out of your clients' money blocks. They will be forever changed, and so will you.

ACKNOWLEDGEMENTS

This book wouldn't have been written if my husband, Pete, wasn't such a brilliant husband and father, capable of holding the fort with one hand, and carrying our toddler around in the other.

My beautiful daughters, Eloisa and Camilla, the best Mastermind buddies an entrepreneur could wish for, who have amazing skills for finding solutions, being creative, and making me laugh.

My boy, Jackson, who completed our family, and whose cuteness is scientifically proven to cause the inability to concentrate on anything.

My dad, Rogan, who listens and encourages every development in my business, even though he still doesn't really understand what I do. He's always demonstrated the important of humour in everything, and especially in the face of disapproval.

My mum, Gayle, whose love of books and learning was imprinted into my DNA, who taught me to read when I was three years old, and who never tired of taking me to the library. Without her dedication to my education, my life would look very different now.

My mate Kim, my biggest cheerleader and partner in crime, the only person in England who knows nearly as much about my business as me, and who always 'gets it' – from my most exciting adventures to my most random humour.

My international soul sisters, Ashley and Amy, whose encouragement of my energy work led to me developing a way of working over Skype. Their support in the crazy summer of 2014 paved a big section of this road, and I can't wait to see where we all end up next.

The 'Netballers', my hilarious, kind and wonderful friends, who let me practise my energy-shifting skills on them in the early days, even though they thought I was mad. Those early case studies and small successes were the foundation of the work I do today.

To all my amazing clients, and members of my programmes, whose enthusiasm for, and dedication to, this work inspires me to keep creating. I appreciate every single one of you, even more than you know. With very special thanks to those who allowed their personal stories to be shared in this book.

Shannon Graham, Visionary Leader, who asked me: "What could you teach people in two days?" and then gave me the strategy to execute when I replied: "I can teach them to do what I do."

Stacy Nelson, Author, who just looked at me, and said: "Wealthology. It's Kinesiology, and money… Wealthology." To which I replied: "You are a fecking genius and I love you."

Adrea Peters, Author and Storyteller, who understood the concept for this book from the second I shared it, and turned my heap of ideas into the skeleton of something worth reading. That's a superpower, right there.

Giovanni Marsico, who teaches the brilliant analogy of the entrepreneur as a provider of a service that helps their clients to be superheroes. In his community, Archangel Academy, I've been fortunate enough to connect with many of the people who have made this book a reality.

And of course, the awesome team at Difference Press, especially Dr. Angela Lauria, and my editor, Cynthia Kane, whose wisdom and guidance meant that I really enjoyed writing this book so much that I'm already planning the next one.

ABOUT THE AUTHOR

Michelle Lowbridge, The Energy Editor®, is one of the most sought-after teachers and healers in Europe. She quickly identifies the money blocks that are stopping an entrepreneur from unleashing their superpower, then smashes them, using her powerful Wealthology® system. Her clients release lifelong patterns, and multiply their income as a result.

In 2014, after years of training and working with hundreds of clients, Michelle closed down her Kinesiology practice. Despite helping many people with many things, she was unable to generate enough revenue to make it worthwhile, and, pregnant with her third child, decided to quit.

Life had other ideas. When baby Jackson was six weeks old, Michelle used her Energy Editing® skills to find and clear her subconscious blocks to money. Within 48 hours, everything changed, and she was suddenly in demand from clients all over the world. Over the next six weeks, her life changed forever.

The business continues to expand, and Michelle now teaches coaches how to smash their clients' money blocks. She is endlessly fascinated with these hidden demons, which limit our ability to create wealth even though we often have no idea that they exist.

Michelle is dedicated to honest conversations about money, creating freedom for herself and her family, and encouraging entrepreneurs to do business in their own way. A journalism graduate from The University of Westminster, she lives in the English countryside, and is a huge fan of Sherlock, the occasional cheeky cocktail, and laughing until she snorts.

Website: www.michellelowbridge.com
Email: michelle@michellelowbridge.com

THANK YOU

Thanks so much for reading. It's been a true pleasure to write this book, and I hope you've enjoyed learning the Wealthology system. You now know what to do to create powerful changes in your clients' relationships to money so that they can enjoy wealth without limits.

I've created a **free Wealthology Toolkit**, packed with practical resources to assist you in your money-block smashing.

Access yours right now at **www.michellelowbridge.com/ wealthologygifts**

Inside you'll find…

Printable Wealthology Profiler
The secret behind the quiz on my website, so you can identify your client's Wealthology Profile in minutes!

Wealthology Insider Secrets

My technique for smashing limiting beliefs in 30 seconds, PLUS the exact limiting belief phrases to use with your clients, for every Wealthology Theme and Profile!

Printable Wealthology Cheat Sheet

An easy-reference guide on how every Wealthology Theme affects each Profile, for when you're in session with your clients!

Just go to **www.michellelowbridge.com/wealthologygifts** and you'll receive the Wealthology Toolkit straight to your inbox.

I'm beyond excited that you now understand the science of smashing money blocks, and this really is just the beginning of what's possible for you and your clients.

With love

Michelle, The Energy Editor

A free eBook edition is available with the purchase of this book.

To claim your free eBook edition:

1. Download the Shelfie app.
2. Write your name in upper case in the box.
3. Use the Shelfie app to submit a photo.
4. Download your eBook to any device.

Shelfie

A free eBook edition is available
with the purchase of this print book.

CLEARLY PRINT YOUR NAME ABOVE IN UPPER CASE

Instructions to claim your free eBook edition:
1. Download the Shelfie app for Android or iOS
2. Write your name in **UPPER CASE** above
3. Use the Shelfie app to submit a photo
4. Download your eBook to any device

Print & Digital Together Forever.

Snap a photo

Free eBook

Read anywhere

www.TheMorganJamesSpeakersGroup.com

We connect Morgan James published
authors with live and online events
and audiences whom will benefit
from their expertise.

Morgan James
Speakers Group

Printed in the USA
CPSIA information can be obtained
at www.ICGtesting.com
JSHW021957150824
68134JS00055B/2080